VAT IN PROPERTY AND CONSTRUCTION

VAT IN PROPERTY AND CONSTRUCTION

Julian Potts

Acknowledgements

Crown copyright material is reproduced with the permission of the Controller of HMSO and the Queen's Printer for Scotland.

Please note: References to the masculine include, where appropriate, the feminine.

Published by RICS Business Services Limited
a wholly owned subsidiary of
The Royal Institution of Chartered Surveyors
under the RICS Books imprint
Surveyor Court
Westwood Business Park
Coventry CV4 8JE
UK

ISBN 1 84219 229 9

Typeset in Great Britain by Columns Design Ltd, Reading
Printed in Great Britain by Bell & Bain Ltd, Glasgow

Contents

Preface   ix

List of European Directives, Acts, Statutory Instruments and
abbreviations   xiii

Table of Cases   xv

1   **General principles**   1
   1.1   What is VAT?   1
   1.2   The legislation   1
      1.2.1   Application of European law   2
   1.3   The basic operation of VAT   3
      1.3.1   Output tax   3
      1.3.2   Input tax   3
      1.3.3   The VAT return   3
      1.3.4   Restrictions on VAT recovery   4
   1.4   The main VAT charging provision   4
   1.5   The concept of supply   5
      1.5.1   Cases where held that a supply was made   5
      1.5.2   Cases where held that no supply was made   6
      1.5.3   Cases regarding deemed supplies   8
      1.5.4   Deemed non-supplies   9
      1.5.5   Consideration   9
   1.6   Profit sharing agreements, partnerships and joint
      ventures   11
   1.7   Goods and services   12
      1.7.1   Goods   12
      1.7.2   Services   13
   1.8   Taxable supplies   14
   1.9   Taxable person   15
      1.9.1   'Taxable person' – UK and European
          definitions   15
          1.9.1.1   UK perspective – business   15
          1.9.1.2   European perspective – economic
               activity   16

Contents

1.9.2	Case law	16
	1.9.2.1 Business	16
	1.9.2.2 Non-business	17
1.9.3	Registration	18
	1.9.3.1 Compulsory registration	18
	1.9.3.2 Voluntary registration	19
	1.9.3.3 Intending trader	19
	1.9.3.4 Pre-registration VAT	20
1.9.4	Deregistration	21
1.9.5	VAT groups	21
1.10	Multiple or compound supplies	22
1.10.1	The current test	22
1.10.2	Composite supplies	23
1.10.3	Multiple supplies	24
1.11	Are the supplies 'made in the UK'?	25
1.11.1	Supplies of goods	25
1.11.2	Supplies of services	27
1.12	Eighth VAT Directive refunds	28
1.13	Thirteenth VAT Directive refunds	28
1.14	Time of supply	28
1.14.1	Construction services	30
1.14.2	Retention payments	30
1.15	Valuation of supplies	31
1.15.1	Discounts	33
1.15.2	Tax deductions	34
1.16	Input tax recovery	34
1.16.1	VAT incurred on non-business activities	35
1.16.2	VAT incurred on taxable or exempt activities	36
1.16.3	Partial exemption	39
1.16.4	Capital Goods Scheme	42
1.16.5	Non-deductible input tax	43
1.17	Tax avoidance	44
1.18	Insolvency	47
1.19	Collection and administration	48
1.19.1	Assessments	49
1.19.2	Penalties	50
1.19.3	VAT rulings	53
1.19.4	Extra-statutory concessions	54
1.19.5	Complaints	55
1.19.6	Disputes	56
1.20	Miscellaneous	57
1.20.1	Interaction with other taxes	57

	1.20.1.1	Taxes generally	57
	1.20.1.2	Stamp Duty Land Tax	57
1.20.2	Damages		58
	1.20.2.1	Liquidated damages	58
	1.20.2.2	Compensation	58
1.21	Local authorities and other governmental bodies		59
1.22	Scottish law		62

2 Commercial property **64**

2.1	Introduction		64
2.2	VAT exempt supplies of land		65
	2.2.1	Licence to occupy	66
2.3	VAT standard-rated supplies of land		70
	2.3.1	Sale of new commercial buildings	71
		2.3.1.1 Definition of civil engineering	71
	2.3.2	Right to take game or fish	72
	2.3.3	Hotels and similar accommodation	73
	2.3.4	Holiday accommodation	76
	2.3.5	Seasonal pitches for caravans, tents or camping facilities	77
	2.3.6	Provision of parking facilities	78
	2.3.7	Right to fell or remove timber	80
	2.3.8	Storage of aircraft and boats	80
	2.3.9	Seats at sports grounds, theatre, concert halls, etc.	80
	2.3.10	Grant of facilities for playing sport	81
	2.3.11	Options	82
2.4	The option to tax		82
	2.4.1	Principles	82
	2.4.2	Making the option to tax	84
	2.4.3	Disapplication of the option to tax	87
2.5	Lease transactions		91
	2.5.1	Variations to leases	97
	2.5.2	Third party costs	97
	2.5.3	Service charges	98
2.6	Transfer of a business as a going concern		99
	2.6.1	Generally	99
	2.6.2	Meaning of 'transfer of a business as a going concern'	100
	2.6.3	Meaning of 'same kind of business'	101
	2.6.4	Meaning of 'notifying an election before the relevant date'	101

Contents

3   Residential and charitable property   103
3.1   Residential development land   103
3.2   The sale and letting of residential property   105
3.3   What is a 'major interest'?   105
3.4   Who is the 'person constructing' the building?   108
3.5   What is a building?   109
3.6   What is a building 'designed as a dwelling'?   111
3.7   What is a 'non-residential' building?   114
3.8   What is a building used for a 'relevant
       residential purpose'?   118
3.9   What is a building used for a 'relevant
       charitable purpose'?   120
       3.9.1   Charitable annexe   123
3.10   What is a 'substantially reconstructed
       protected building'?   125
       3.10.1 Protected building   125
       3.10.2 Substantially reconstructed   125
3.11   Change of qualifying use   127

4   Construction services   128
4.1   New buildings   128
4.2   Works 'in the course of construction'   129
4.3   Building materials   133
4.4   Construction services to existing buildings   136
       4.4.1   Housing association conversions   136
       4.4.2   Approved alterations to protected buildings   137
               4.4.2.1   Protected buildings   137
               4.4.2.2   Approved alterations   138
               4.4.2.3   Crown or Duchy buildings   138
               4.4.2.4   Listed places of worship   141
       4.4.3   Adaptations for disabled persons   142
4.5   Supply of 'relevant goods' to an 'eligible body'   145
4.6   VAT reduced-rate construction services   146
       4.6.1   Residential conversions   147
       4.6.2   Residential renovations and alterations   147
       4.6.3   Energy-saving materials   149
       4.6.4   Grant-funded installation of heating
               equipment, security goods, or
               connection of gas supply   150
4.7   DIY house-builders and converters   150
4.8   Services of consultants   152
4.9   Miscellaneous matters   153

Index   155

Preface

While chartered surveyors may not need the *breadth* of understanding of the law of their opposite numbers in the legal profession, there are a number of key areas of application to property and construction where they need a similar *depth* of legal knowledge. Exactly what the key areas may be depends to some extent on the nature of the surveyor's practice. Two obvious examples are the law relating to landlord and tenant and to town and country planning. There are plenty of chartered surveyors who know much more about rent reviews or compulsory purchase compensation than the average lawyer in general practice. They need to know the law as much as the valuation principles, not least because the former can affect the latter.

Surveyors, therefore, require legal knowledge and for a variety of reasons need to develop their understanding of the law. Changing trends or individual variations in clients' requirements mean that from time to time even the best practitioners (perhaps, especially, the best practitioners) will feel the need to expand their knowledge. The knowledge acquired at college or in studying for the Assessment of Professional Competence has a limited shelf-life and needs to be constantly updated to maintain its currency. Even specialists working in their areas of expertise need a source of reference as an aide-mémoire or as a first port of call in more detailed research.

The Case in Point series

RICS Books is committed to meeting the needs of surveying (and other) professionals and the Case in Point series typifies that commitment. It is aimed at those who need to upgrade or update their legal knowledge, or who need to have access to a good first reference at the outset of an inquiry. A particular difficulty in doing so lies in the area of case law. There are few legal subjects of interest to surveyors where case law does not play a major role. This is true of areas such as professional negligence, largely ungoverned by statute, where the cases constitute the law. However, it is also true of subjects like landlord and tenant and town and country planning, where a statutory framework exists but where the interpretation and application of the provisions at the sharp end are provided by judicial decisions. Chartered surveyors are generally well aware of the importance of case law but are confronted by a significant practical problem in dealing with it, namely, the burgeoning of reported decisions of the courts. The sheer scale of the law reports, both general and specialist, makes it very hard even to be aware of recent trends, let alone identify the significance of a particular decision. Thus it was decided to focus on the developments in case law. In any given matter, the practitioner will want to be directed efficiently and painlessly to the decision which bears upon the matter which he or she is dealing with; in other words, to the 'case in point'.

The Case in Point series offers a wealth of legal information, which is essential in its practical application to the surveyor's work. The author of each title has the degree of expertise required to be selective and succinct; thus achieving a high level of relevancy without sacrificing accessibility. The series has developed incrementally and now comprises a collection of specialist handbooks which can deliver what busy practitioners need – the law on the matter they are handling, when they want it.

VAT Case in Point

Originating from European legislation, value added tax (VAT) is now firmly established as one of the principal forms of taxation in the UK. It is certainly one of the most pervasive taxes, being charged on all stages of production and distribution in the provision of goods and services across a huge range of areas of activity. It is thus unsurprising that VAT has a significant and often decisive impact on the economics of property development and construction. For this reason practising quantity surveyors, and other construction and property professionals, have to acquire familiarity with the VAT regime. They may not each need to become experts – a number of specialists fulfil this need, of whom the author of this work is one – but they must have a firm grasp of the basic concepts and know where to check on whether, for example, a supply for VAT purposes has been made or not. Whether a project or a building falls within or outwith the scope of the tax can make the difference between its viability and non-viability. For example, a property transaction which is classified as VAT exempt would mean that no VAT expenditure on the building in question is recoverable.

Given the stakes, it is not surprising that numerous battles have been fought on applicability of VAT, on exempt supply or non-exempt supply, zero-rating or non zero-rating. There is a mass of case law. The practitioner needs to be guided through it in order to see what decisions exist; at best to find the answer, at worst to see if there is an issue to be resolved.

Julian Potts is well qualified for the task of guide. He is an ideal combination of VAT expert and chartered surveyor. An ATT-qualified tax specialist and professional member of the VAT Practitioners Group, Julian runs a company, Landmark PT, which provides tax advice to the construction and property industries. But he is also an experienced construction and property practitioner himself. A chartered quantity surveyor, his specialism is the effect of VAT on residential and commercial property development. Julian sits as a member of the British Property Federation's VAT committee and the RICS Tax Policy panel. He brings extensive knowledge and also practical experience to the task of organising and explaining the case law on VAT and this combination explains his success in doing so.

Anthony Lavers, 2005.
Professional Support Lawyer, White & Case, London.
Visiting Professor of Law, Oxford Brookes University, Oxford.
Consultant Editor, Case in Point Series.

List of European Directives, Acts, Statutory Instruments and abbreviations

The following European Directives, Acts and Statutory Instruments are referenced in this publication. Where a European Directive or Act is mentioned frequently, it is referred to by the abbreviation in brackets that follows.

First Council Directive of the European Union (77/227/EEC)
(**'First VAT Directive'**)
Second Council Directive of the European Union (67/227/EEC)
(**'Second VAT Directive'**)
Sixth Council Directive of the European Union (77/388/EEC)
(**'Sixth VAT Directive'**)
Eighth Council Directive of the European Union (79/1072/EEC)
Thirteenth Council Directive of the European Union (86/560/EEC)

Agricultural Tenancies Act 1995
Ancient Monuments and Archaeological Areas Act 1979
Chronically Sick and Disabled Persons Act 1970
Historic Monuments and Archaeological Objects (Northern Ireland) Order 1995 (SI 1995/1625) (N.I.9)
Housing (Northern Ireland) Order 1992 (SI 1992/1725) (N.I.15)
Housing (Scotland) Act 1987
Housing Act 1988
Housing Act 1996
Housing Associations Act 1985
Income and Corporation Taxes Act 1988
Landlord and Tenant Act 1954
Planning (Listed Buildings and Conservation Areas) (Scotland) Act 1997
Planning (Listed Buildings and Conservation Areas) Act 1990

Planning (Northern Ireland) Order 1991 (SI 1991 / 1220) (N.I.11)
Value Added Tax (Self-supply of Construction Services) Order 1989
(SI 1989 / 472)
Value Added Tax Act 1994 ('**VAT Act 1994**')
Value Added Tax Regulations 1995, (SI 1995 / 2518) ('**VAT
Regulations 1995**')
Value Added Tax (Construction of Buildings) Order 1995, (SI 1995 / 280)
Value Added Tax (Registered Social Landlords) (No. 1) Order 1997,
(SI 1997 / 50)
Value Added Tax (Conversion of Buildings) Order 2001, (SI 2001 / 2305)
Value Added Tax (Construction of Buildings) Order 2002,
(SI 2002 / 1101)

The text of this publication is divided into commentary and case
summaries. The commentary is enclosed between grey highlighted
lines for ease of reference.

Table of Cases

22a Property Investments Ltd, VAT Decision No. 14544;
[1997] BVC 2,077 14
2S Airchangers Ltd, VAT Decision No. 12495; [1995] BVC
1,525 135

Abbottsley Golf & Squash Club Ltd, VAT Decision
No. 15042; [1997] BVC 2,492 69
Acorn Management Services Ltd, VAT Decision
No. 17338; [2001] BVC 2,388 75
Adams, VAT Decision No. 18054; [2003] BVC 4,099 139
AE House & Son, VAT Decision No. 2620; (1988)
3 BVC 695 78
Agudas Israel Housing Association Ltd, VAT Decision
No. 18798; [2005] BVC 4,029 113
Alan Roper & Sons Ltd, VAT Decision No. 15260; [1998]
BVC 4,039 139
Alexander, VAT Decision No. 4560; (1990) 5 BVC 1,313 . 152
All Saints with St Nicholas Church, VAT Decision
No. 16321; [2000] BVC 4,039 139
Amicus Group Ltd, VAT Decision No. 17693; [2003]
BVC 4,005 117
Archer v C & E Commrs (1974) VATTR 1 18
Ashworth, VAT Decision No. 12924; [1996] BVC 2,110 .. 77
Aspen Advisory Services Ltd, VAT Decision No. 13489;
[1996] BVC 2,456 27
Avis (t/a Property Alterations), VAT Decision No. 10664;
[1994] BVC 1,337 144

BAA v C & E Commrs [1997] STC 36 69
Beaverbank Properties Ltd, VAT Decision No. 18099;
[2003] V & DR 538; [2003] BVC 4,108 39
Becker v Finanzamt Munster-Innenstadt (Case 8/81)
[1982] ECR 53, [1982] 1 CMLR 499 (ECJ) 2
Beco Products Ltd, VAT Decision No. 18638; [2004] BVC
4,100 150

Belgian State v Ghent Coal Terminal NV (Case C-37/95)
[1998] ECR I-1; [1998] BVC 139; [1998] STC 260 (ECJ)   37
Belvedere Properties (Cheltenham) Ltd, VAT Decision
No. 18851; [2005] BVC 4,043   118
Bird Semple & Crawford Herron, VAT Decision No. 2171;
(1986) VATTR 218; (1986) 2 BVC 205,488   12
Birmingham Council for Old People, VAT Decision
No. 15437; [1998] BVC 4,086   134
BJ Group Ltd, VAT Decision No. 18234; [2003] BVC 2,614   76
Blasi v Finanzamt München I (Case C-346/95) [1998]
ECR I-481; [1998] BVC 247; [1998] STC 336 (ECJ)   65
Blendhome Ltd (t/a Stanhill Court Hotel), VAT Decision
No. 16048; [1999] BVC 2,280 . . . .   24, 70
BLP Group plc v C & E Commrs (Case C-4/94) [1995]
ECR I-983; [1995] BVC 159; [1995] STC 424 (ECJ)   35
Blythe Limited Partnership, VAT Decision No. 16011;
[1999] BVC 2,224   85
Boys' and Girls' Welfare Society, VAT Decision No. 15274;
[1998] BVC 2,070   144
Brambletye School Trust Ltd, VAT Decision No. 17688;
[2003] BVC 2,015   90
Brand (as Trustee of Racket Sports for Children with
Special Needs), VAT Decision No. 14080; [1996]
BVC 4,290   144
Brice, VAT Decision No. 6376; [1991] BVC 828   140
British Telecommunications plc, VAT Decision No. 16244;
[2000] BVC 2,086   70
Broadhurst (t/a RMS Heating), VAT Decision No. 2007;
(1985) 2 BVC 208,084   8
Brodrick Wright & Strong Ltd, VAT Decision No. 2347;
(1987) 3 BVC 1,318   27
Bruce, VAT Decision No. 6326; [1991] BVC 798   110
Buckley (t/a Wheelcraft Centre & Original Homes),
VAT Decision No. 7150; [1992] BVC 1,414   39
Burgess (t/a Cards n Cuddles), VAT Decision No. 14475;
[1997] BVC 4,008   25
Business Enterprises (UK) Ltd, VAT Decision No. 3161;
(1988) VATTR 160; (1988) 3 BVC 854 . . . . 68, 98, 153

Calam Vale Ltd, VAT Decision No. 16869; [2001]
BVC 4,056   116
Cantrell (t/a Foxearth Lodge Nursing Home) v
C & E Commrs [2003] EWHC 404 (Ch); [2003]
BVC 196; [2003] STC 486 (ChD)   111

Card Protection Plan Ltd v C & E Commrs
(Case C-349/96) [1999] BVC I-973; [1999] BVC 155 . . .   22
Carlton Lodge Club v C & E Commrs [1974] 3 All ER 798;
(1974) 1 BVC 16; [1974] STC 507   5
Carter, VAT Decision No. 17288; [2001] BVC 4,157   72
Castle Caereinion Recreation Association, VAT Decision
No. 18303; [2004] BVC 4,019   124
Central Capital Corporation Ltd, VAT Decision No. 13319;
[1996] BVC 2,336   96
Centralan Property Ltd v C & E Commrs [2003] EWHC 44
(Ch); [2003] BVC 187; [2003] STC 290; (ChD)   43
Centrax Ltd, VAT Decision No. 15743; [1998] V & DR 369;
[1999] BVC 2,057   26
Chalegrove Properties Ltd, VAT Decision No. 17151;
[2001] V & DR 316; [2001] BVC 2,279 . . . .   84, 101
Chalk Springs Fisheries, VAT Decision No. 2518; (1987)
3 BVC 1,341   73
Cheshire Chimneys, VAT Decision No. 5112; (1990)
5 BVC 794   5
Chipping Sodbury Town Trust, VAT Decision No. 16641;
[2000] BVC 2,386   132
Church Schools Foundation Ltd v C & E Commrs [2002]
BVC 114; [2001] STC 1661 (CA)   7
Classic Furniture (Newport) Ltd, VAT Decision No. 16977;
[2001] BVC 4,081   86
Clean Car Co Ltd, VAT Decision No. 5695; [1991]
BVC 568   29
Clowance Holdings Ltd, VAT Decision No. 17289; [2001]
BVC 4,157   23
Clowance Owners Club Ltd, VAT Decision No. 18787;
[2005] BVC 2,169   99
Coach House Property Management Ltd, VAT Decision
No. 7564; [1992] BVC 1,485   83
Colaingrove Ltd v C & E Commrs [2004] EWCA
Civ 146   78
Colchester School of Gymnastics, VAT Decision
No. 15370   81
Cooke, VAT Decision No. 1844; (1985) 3 BVC 208,063 . .   31
Cooper & Chapman (Builders) Ltd v C & E Commrs
[1993] BVC 11; [1993] STC 1 (QB)   41
Cooper Chasney Ltd, VAT Decision No. 4898; (1990)
5 BVC 677   59

Cumbernauld Development Corporation, VAT Decision
No. 14630; [1997] BVC 4,043   10
C & E Commrs v Arbib [1995] BVC 201; [1995] STC 490 .   140
C & E Commrs v Barclays Bank plc [2001] STC 1558 . . .   22
C & E Commrs v Battersea Leisure Ltd [1992] BVC 23;
[1993] STC 213   32
C & E Commrs v Briararch Ltd [1992] BVC 118; [1992]
STC 732 . . . . 14, 37, 106
C & E Commrs v Cantor Fitzgerald International
(Case C-108/99) [2001] ECR I-7257; [2002] BVC 9;
[2001] STC 1453 (ECJ)   97
C & E Commrs v Croyden Hotel and Leisure Co Ltd
[1996] BVC 394; [1996] STC 1105   50
C & E Commrs v Curtis Henderson Ltd [1992] BVC 118;
[1992] STC 732   37
C & E Commrs v Deutsche Ruck UK Reinsurance
Co Ltd [1995] BVC 175; [1995] STC 495 (QB)   40
C & E Commrs v Jacobs [2004] BVC 835; [2004] STC 1662
(ChD)   117
C & E Commrs v Jeffs (t/a J & J Joinery) [1995] BVC 302;
[1995] STC 759 . . . .   24, 135
C & E Commrs v Kingfisher [1994] BVC 3; [1994]
STC 63   21
C & E Commrs v Latchmere Properties Ltd [2005]
EWHC 133 (Ch); [2005] All ER (D) 142 (Feb) (ChD) . .   11
C & E Commrs v Link Housing Association Ltd [1992]
BVC 113; [1992] STC 718   108
C & E Commrs v Lord Fisher (1981) 1 BVC 392; [1981]
STC 238 (QB) 17, 73
C & E Commrs v McLean Homes Midland Ltd [1993]
BVC 99; [1993] STC 335   134
C & E Commrs v Mirror Group plc (Case C-409/98)
[2001] ECR I-7175; [2002] BVC 16 (ECJ)   93
C & E Commrs v Morrison's Academy Boarding Houses
Association 1977 SLT 197; (1977) 1 BVC 108; [1978]
STC 1 . . . .   16, 121
C & E Commrs v Oliver [1980] 1 All ER 354; (1979)
1 BVC 314; [1980] STC 73   13
C & E Commrs v Parkinson (1988) 3 BVC 303; [1989]
STC 51   73
C & E Commrs v Rannoch School Ltd [1993] BVC 118;
[1993] STC 389   130

C & E Commrs v R & R Pension Fund Trustees [1996]
BVC 348; [1996] STC 889 85
C & E Commrs v Redrow Group Ltd [1999] BVC 96;
[1999] STC 161 35
C & E Commrs v Sinclair Collis Ltd (Case C-275/01)
[2003] ECR I-5965; [2003] BVC 374 (ECJ) 67
C & E Commrs v Southern Primary Housing Ltd [2004]
BVC 88; [2004] STC 209 .... 38, 104
C & E Commrs v St Mary's Roman Catholic High School
[1996] BVC 373; [1996] STC 1091 130
C & E Commrs v St Paul's Community Project Ltd [2005]
BVC 12 (ChD) 121
C & E Commrs v Steptoe [1992] BVC 142; [1992] STC 757
(CA) 53
C & E Commrs v The David Lewis Centre [1995] BVC 188;
[1995] STC 485 (QB) 146
C & E Commrs v Trinity Factoring Services Ltd [1994]
BVC 169; [1994] STC 504 79
C & E Commrs v University of Wales College of Cardiff
[1995] BVC 211; [1995] STC 611 86
C & E Commrs v Wiggett Construction [2002] BVC 3;
[2001] STC 933 .... 38, 104
C & E Commrs v Windflower Housing Association [1995]
BVC 329 140
C & E Commrs v Yarburgh Children's Trust [2002]
BVC 141 (ChD) 121
C & E Commrs v Zielinski Baker & Partners Ltd [2004]
UKHL 7; [2004] STC 456 (HL); [2002] BVC 525 (CA) . 138

D Dyball & Son, VAT Decision No. 4863; (1990)
5 BVC 667 36
Dart Major Works Ltd, VAT Decision No. 18781; [2005]
BVC 2,105 .... 131, 139
David Grey Homes & Gardens Ltd, VAT Decision
No. 2624; (1988) 3 BVC 690 36
Davison, VAT Decision No. 17130; [2001] BVC 4,115 114
DCM Leisure Ltd, VAT Decision No. 16966; [2001]
BVC 4,078 8
Denman College, VAT Decision No. 15513; [1998]
BVC 2,259 119
Dinaro Ltd (t/a Fairway Lodge), VAT Decision
No. 17148; [2001] BVC 4,120 75

Dormers Builders (London) Ltd v C & E Commrs (1989)
BVC 111 (CA) 29

East Kent Medical Services Ltd, VAT Decision No. 16095;
[1999] BVC 2,299 90
EC Commission v United Kingdom (Case 416/85) [1988]
ECR 3127; (1988) 3 BVC 378; [1988] STC 456 (ECJ) ... 2
EC Commission v United Kingdom (Case C-359/97)
[2000] ECR I-6355; [2001] BVC 458; [2000] STC 777
(ECJ) 65
Edmond Homes Ltd, VAT Decision No. 11567; [1995]
BVC 1,368 134
Electric Tool Repair Ltd, VAT Decision No. 2208; (1986)
2 BVC 205,478 53
Elliot, VAT Decision No. 4926; (1990) 5 BVC 1,361 20
Elstead (Thursley Road) Recreational Trust,
VAT Decision No. 18852; [2005] BVC 4,043 54
Enever, VAT Decision No. 1537; (1986) 2 BVC 208,026 .. 68
Erinmore Homes Ltd, VAT Decision No. 17233; [2001]
BVC 4,144 135
ES Poyser & Sons Ltd v Capital & Counties plc (1991)
Nottingham County Court Case No. 89/75411 32
Evans, VAT Decision No. 4415; (1989) 4 BVC 1,443 ..... 139, 140
Evans, VAT Decision No. 17264; [2001] BVC 4,152 111

F & I Services Ltd v C & E Commrs [2001] BVC 347;
[2001] STC 939 (CA) 54
Fforestfach Medical Centre, VAT Decision No. 16587;
[2000] BVC 4,100 91
Finanzamt Goslar v Breitsohl (Case C-400/98) [2000]
ECR I-4321; [2001] STC 355 (ECJ) 83
Finanzamt Uelzen v Armbrecht (Case C-291/92) [1995]
I-ECR 2775; [1995] All ER 882; [1995] STC 997 (ECJ) .. 18, 84
First Base Properties Ltd, VAT Decision No. 11598;
[1995] BVC 1,374 23
Fivegrange Ltd, VAT Decision No. 5338; (1990)
5 BVC 1,417 11
Flynn, VAT Decision No. 16930; [2001] BVC 4,069 152
Fonden Marselisborg Lystbådehavn v Skatteministeriet
(Case C-428/02) 3 March 2005 (not yet reported) 79
Franks & Collingwood v Gates (1985) 1 Con LR 21 32
Furniss v Dawson [1984] AC 474; [1984] STC 153 45

Garnham (t/a Pro-Mac Surfacing), VAT Decision
    No. 15918; [1999] BVC 4,059   58

General Healthcare Group Ltd, VAT Decision No. 17129;
    [2001] BVC 4,114 119

Georgiou (t/a Marios's Chippery) v United Kingdom
    [2001] STC 80   51

Gilbourne, VAT Decision No. 109; (1974) VATTR 209 . . . 131

GKN Birwelco Ltd, VAT Decision No. 1430; (1983)
    VATTR 128; (1983) 2 BVC 208,014   71

Glasgow City Council, VAT Decision No. 15491; [1998]
    V & DR 407; [1998] BVC 2,239   60

Gleneagles Hotel plc, VAT Decision No. 2512; (1986)
    VATTR 196; (1985) 2 BVC 208,108   94

Glenrothes Development Corp v IR Commrs [1994]
    BTC 8,019; [1994] STC 74   57

Glenshane Construction Services Ltd (in liquidation),
    VAT Decision No. 14160; [1996] BVC 4,308   48

Goldmax Resources Ltd, VAT Decision No. 18219; [2003]
    BVC 4,140 104

Grace Baptist Church, VAT Decision No. 16093; [1999]
    BVC 2,294 123

Greater World Association Trust (Trustees for),
    VAT Decision No. 3401; (1989) VATTR 91; (1989)
    4 BVC 607   31

GT Scaffolding Ltd, VAT Decision No. 18225; [2003]
    BVC 4,143 131

Halifax plc, VAT Decision No. 17124; [2001] BVC 2,240 .   46

Hammersmith & West London College, VAT Decision
    No. 17540; [2002] BVC 2,102   85

Hardy, VAT Decision No. 12776; [1994] VATTR 302;
    [1996] BVC 2,057 141

Haven Leisure Ltd, VAT Decision No. 5269; (199)
    5 BVC 844   76

Heijn, VAT Decision No. 15562; [1998] BVC 4,121 141

Henley Picture House Ltd BIR/79/107 (1979)
    VAT Decision 895   79

Higher Education Statistics Agency Ltd v C & E Commrs
    [2000] BVC 150; [2000] STC 332 (QB) 101

Holiday Inns (UK) Ltd, VAT Decision No. 10609; [1994]
    BVC 543   58

Holmwood House School Developments, VAT Decision
    No. 18130; [2003] BVC 2,532 . . . . 69, 90

Hordern, VAT Decision No. 8941; [1993] BVC 613   19
Hostgilt Ltd v Megahart [1999] BVC 78; [1999] STC 141 .   33
House (t/a P & J Autos) v C & E Commrs [1996]
    BVC 116; (1995) STI 1669   49
Hulme Trust Educational Foundation Trustees,
    VAT Decision No. 625; (1978) 1 BVC 1,083   108

Ian Flockton Developments Ltd v C & E Commrs (1987)
    3 BVC 23; [1987] STC 394   36
Iliffe, VAT Decision No. 10922; [1993] VATTR 439; [1994]
    BVC 625   7
Inchcape Management Services Ltd, VAT Decision
    No. 16256; [2000] BVC 2,104   50
IR Commrs v Challenge Corp Ltd [1987] AC 155; [1986]
    STC 548   45
IR Commrs v Duke of Westminster [1936] AC 1   45
Inter City Motor Auctions Ltd, VAT Decision No. 2319;
    (1987) 3 BVC 571   80
Intercommunale voor Zeewaterontzilting (INZO) v
    Belgian State (Case C-110/94) [1996] ECR I-857; [1996]
    BVC 326 (ECJ)   20
International Students House, VAT Decision No. 14420;
    [1996] BVC 2,975   74
Isaac, VAT Decision No. 14656; [1997] BVC 2,175   15
Isle of Wight Council, VAT Decision No. 18557; [2004]
    EWHC 2541 (Ch); [2005] BVC 228   61
I/S Fini H v Skatteministeriet (Case C-32/03) [2005]
    All ER (D) 62 (Mar) (ECJ)   36

Jaymarke Developments v Elinacre Ltd (in liquidation)
    [1992] BVC 67; [1992] STC 575   33
Jenkinson, VAT Decision No. 2688; (1988) 3 BVC 729 ...   53
J Hopkins (Contractors) Ltd, VAT Decision No. 3511;
    (1989) 4 BVC 619; (1989) VATTR 107   6
JM Associates, VAT Decision No. 18624; [2004]
    BVC 4,098   131
Johnsen (Chairman of Shalden Millennium Committee),
    VAT Decision No. 17897; [2003] BVC 4,059   144
Johnson, VAT Decision No. 16672; [2001] BVC 4,008   144
Jones, VAT Decision No. 12339; [1995] BVC 1,497   44
Jubilee Hall Recreation Centre v C & E Commrs [1999]
    BVC 184; [1999] STC 381   122

KapHag Renditefonds 35 Spreecenter Berlin-Hellersdorf 3.
  Tanche GbR v Finanzamt Charlottenburg
  (Case C-442/01) [2003] ECR I-6851; [2003] All ER (D)
  362 (Jun) (ECJ)   7
Keeping Newcastle Warm v C & E Commrs
  (Case C-353/00) [2002] ECR I-5419; [2003] BVC 283;
  [2002] STC 943 (ECJ)   10
Keydon Estates Ltd, VAT Decision No. 4471; (1990)
  5 BVC 512   6
Kingscastle Ltd, VAT Decision No. 17777; [2003]
  BVC 4,027   117
Kretztechnik AG v Finanzamt Linz (Case C-465/03)
  26 May 2005 (not yet reported)   8
Kwik Save Group plc, VAT Decision No. 12749; [1996]
  BVC 4,004   101

Lambert's Construction Ltd, VAT Decision No. 8882;
  [1993] BVC 1,319   130
Lancer UK Ltd, VAT Decision No. 2070; (1986)
  VATTR 112; (1986) 2 BVC 208,094   146
Laurie (t/a The Peacock Montessori Nursery),
  VAT Decision No. 17219; [2001] BVC 2,317   46
League of Friends of Kingston Hospital, VAT Decision
  No. 12764; [1996] BVC 2,039   122
Leeds and Holbeck Building Society, VAT Decision
  No. 15356; [1998] BVC 4,066   48
Leez Priory, VAT Decision No. 18185; [2003] BVC 4,131 .   75
Lincoln Oak Co Ltd, VAT Decision No. 18503; [2004]
  BVC 4,072   149
Livingstone Homes UK Ltd, VAT Decision No. 16649;
  [2000] BVC 2,400 ....   77, 107
Loch Tay Highland Lodges Ltd, VAT Decision No. 18785;
  [2005] BVC 4,026 ....   77, 107
London Borough of Haringey v C & E Commrs (and
  cross-appeal) [1995] BVC 314; [1995] STC 830 (QB) ..   60
Look Ahead Housing and Care Ltd, VAT Decision
  No. 16816; [2001] BVC 2,107   116
Lordsregal Ltd, VAT Decision No. 18535; [2004]
  BVC 2,144   127
Lounds (t/a Lounds Associates), VAT Decision No.
  13999; [1996] BVC 4,271   88
Love v Norman Wright Builders Ltd [1944] KB 484   32

Lubbock Fine & Co v C & E Commrs (Case C-63/92)
[1993] ECR I-6665; [1993] BVC 287; [1994] STC 101
(ECJ) 67, 95, 96

Macnamara, VAT Decision No. 16039; [1999]
BVC 4,092   124
MacNiven v Westmoreland Investments Ltd [2001]
2 WLR 377; [2001] STC 237   45
Marbourne Ltd, VAT Decision No. 12670; [1995]
BVC 1,222   96
Margrie Holdings Ltd v C & E Commrs (199) 5 BVC 170;
[1991] STC 80   63
McCarthy & Stone plc, VAT Decision No. 7014; [1992]
BVC 1,390   136
McCarthy (t/a Croft Homes), VAT Decision No. 16789;
[2001] BVC 4,038   135
McElroy, VAT Decision No. 490; (1977) 1 BVC 1,066   130
McGrath v C & E Commrs [1992] BVC 51; [1992]
STC 371 (QB)   74
McLean & Gibson (Engineers) Ltd, VAT Decision No.
17500; [2002] BVC 4,033   28
Mechanical Engineering Consultants Ltd, VAT Decision
No. 13287; [1996] BVC 2,289   28
Mellerstain Trust (Trustees of), VAT Decision No. 4256;
(1989) 4 BVC 768   18
Menzies, VAT Decision No. 15733; [1999] BVC 4,015   111
Mercantile Contracts Ltd, VAT Decision No. 4357; (1989)
4 BVC 1,437   30
ME Smith (Electrical Engineers) Ltd, VAT Decision
No. 13594; [1996] BVC 4,180   132
Midgley, VAT Decision No. 15379; [1998] BVC 4,071   110
Mol v Inspecteur der Invoerrechten en Accijnzen
(Case 269/86) [1988] ECR 3627; (1989) 4 BVC 205
(ECJ)   6
Monoprio, VAT Decision No. 17806; [2003] BVC 4,035 . .   148
Moores Furniture Group Ltd, VAT Decision No. 15044;
[1997] BVC 4,137   134

Namecourt Ltd, VAT Decision No. 1560; (1984) VATTR 22;
(1984) 2 BVC 208,028   74
National Provincial Bank Ltd v Ainsworth [1965] AC 1175;
[1965] 3 WLR 1   66

National Society for the Prevention of Cruelty to
Children, VAT Decision No. 9325; [1993] BVC 701;
[1993] STC 275 17
National Westminster Bank plc, VAT Decision No. 15514;
[1998] BVC 2,264 22
Navydock Ltd, VAT Decision No. 18281; [2004]
BVC 4,014 59
Naylor, VAT Decision No. 17305; [2001] BVC 4,162 111
Neal v C & E Commrs (1987) 3 BVC 143; [1988]
STC 131 53
Neville Russell, VAT Decision No. 2484; (1987)
VATTR 194; (1987) 3 BVC 611 94
Newnham College, VAT Decision No. 18936 (not yet
reported) 91
Norbury Developments v C & E Commrs
(Case C-136/97) [1999] ECR I-2491; [1999] BVC 270;
[1999] STC 511 (ECJ)........................... 85
North East Direct Access Ltd, VAT Decision No. 18267;
[2004] BVC 4,008 76

Oldrings Development Kingsclere Ltd, VAT Decision
No. 17769; [2003] BVC 4,025 113

Park Avenue Methodist Church (Trustees of),
VAT Decision No. 17443; [2002] BVC 4,021 20
Peddars Way Housing Association Ltd, VAT Decision
No. 12663; [1995] BVC 1,218 108
Pegasus Birds Ltd v C & E Commrs [2000]
BVC 68 (CA) 50
Peter Anthony Estate Ltd, VAT Decision No. 13250;
[1996] BVC 4,103 99
Poladon Ltd, VAT Decision No. 16825; [2000]
BVC 4,046 98
Poole Borough Council, VAT Decision No. 7180; [1992]
BVC 755 76
Port Erin Hotels Ltd, VAT Decision No. 5045; (1990)
5 BVC 772 95
Pritchard (t/a Dace at 8), VAT Decision No. 18019;
[2003] BVC 4,090 82

R v C & E Commrs, ex parte Greenwich Property Ltd
[2001] EWHC Admin 230; [2001] BVC 261; [2001]
STC 618 (QB) 55

R v Goodwin and Unstead [1997] BVC 307; [1997]
  STC 22 (CA)   6
R & M Scaffolding Ltd, VAT Decision No. 18955
  (not yet reported)   132
Rampling, VAT Decision No. 2067; (1986) VATTR 62;
  (1986) 2 BVC 205,438   29
Ramsay v IR Commrs [1982] AC 300; [1981] STC 174 . . .   45
Rawlins Davy & Wells, VAT Decision No. 523; (1978)
  1 BVC 1,072   72
Rayner & Keeler Ltd v C & E Commrs [1994] BVC 194;
  [1994] STC 724   24
RBS Property Developments Ltd; Royal Bank of Scotland
  Group plc, VAT Decision No. 17789; [2003]
  BVC 2,074   46
Rhondda Cynon Taff County Borough Council,
  VAT Decision No. 16496; [2000] V & DR 149; [2000]
  BVC 2,226   61
Rialto Homes plc, VAT Decision No. 16340; [2000]
  BVC 2,161 . . . . 44, 136
Richard Haynes Associates, VAT Decision No. 12300;
  [1995] BVC 1,054   23
Richards, VAT Decision No. 2355; (1987) 3 BVC 1,319 . . .   13, 59
Ridgeons Bulk Ltd v C & E Commrs [1994] BVC 77;
  [1994] STC 427 (QB) 10, 95
Rochdale Hornets Football Club Co Ltd (1975)
  VATTR 71; (1975) 1 BVC 1,032   67
Rompelman & another v Minister van Financiën
  (Case 268/83) [1985] ECR 655; (1985) 2 BVC 200,157
  (ECJ)   19
Roskill, VAT Decision No. 305; (1981) VATTR 199   72
Routledge, VAT Decision No. 18395; [2004] BVC 4,042 . .   80
Royal & Sun Alliance Group plc v C & E Commrs [2002]
  BVC 174; [2001] STC 1476   38
Royal Midland Counties Home for Disabled People v
  C & E Commrs [2001] BVC 599; [2002] STC 395 (ChD)   146
Royal Sun Alliance Group Insurance Group plc v
  C & E Commrs [2003] UKHL 29; [2003] BVC 341;
  [2003] STC 832   86

Sargent v C & E Commrs [1995] BVC 108; [1995]
  STC 398   48
Sawyer, VAT Decision No. 18872; [2005] BVC 4,048   18

Seaton Parochial Church Council, VAT Decision
No. 18742; [2005] BVC 4,016   13
SEH Holdings Ltd, VAT Decision No. 16771; [2001]
BVC 2,093   88
Severnside Siren Trust Ltd, VAT Decision No. 16640;
[2000] V & DR 497; [2000] BVC 2,381   146
Sheffield Co-operative Society Ltd, VAT Decision
No. 2549; (1987) VATTR 216; (1987) 3 BVC 1,345   40
Sheldon School, VAT Decision No. 15300; [1998]
BVC 4,054   135
Shingler Risdon Associates, VAT Decision No. 2981;
(1988) 3 BVC 822   13
Shiri Guru Nanaka Sikh Temple, VAT Decision
No. 14972; [1997] BVC 4,121   124
Simister, VAT Decision No. 12715; [1995] BVC 1,564   132
Skatteministeriet v Henriksen (Case 173/88) [1989]
ECR 2763; (1990) 5 BVC 140; [1990] STC 768 (ECJ) . . .   79
Smith, VAT Decision No. 13052; [1996] BVC 4,062   78
Softley Ltd (t/a Softley Kitchens), VAT Decision
No. 15034; [1997] BVC 4,136   25
Soka Gakkai International UK, VAT Decision No. 14175;
[1996] BVC 4,311   74
Somerset Car Sales Ltd, VAT Decision No. 11986; [1995]
BVC 1,440   26
Southampton Leisure Holdings, VAT Decision No. 17716;
[2003] BVC 4,010   41
South Aston Community Association, VAT Decision
No. 17702; [2003] BVC 4,007   122
Southend United Football Club, VAT Decision No. 15109;
[1997] V & DR 202; [1998] BVC 2,010   80
Sovereign Street Workspace Ltd, VAT Decision No. 9550;
[1993] BVC 1,452   69
Spijkers v Gebroeders Benedik Abattoir (Case 24/85)
[1986] ECR 1119 (ECJ)   100
Staatssecretaris van Financiën v Coffeeshop Siberië vof
(Case C-158/98) [1999] ECR I-3971; [1999] BVC 353;
[1999] STC 742 (ECJ)   67
Staatssecretaris van Financiën v Coöperatieve
Aardappelenbewaarplaats GA (Case 154/80) [1981]
ECR 445; [1981] 3 CMLR 337 (ECJ)   10
Staatssecretaris van Financiën v Heerma (Case C-23/98)
[2000] ECR I-419; [2003] BVC 97; [2001] STC 1437
(ECJ)   16

Stapenhill Developments Ltd, VAT Decision No. 1593;
(1984) 2 BVC 205,041   109
St Aubyn's School (Woodford Green) Trust Ltd,
VAT Decision No. 1361; (1983) 3 BVC 208,007   72
Stevenson and Telford Building & Design Ltd v
C & E Commrs [1995] BVC 254; [1995] STC 667
(QB)   51
Stichting "Goed Wonen" v Staatssecretaris van
Financiën (Case C-326/99) [2001] ECR I-6831; [2002]
BVC 46; [2003] STC 1137 (ECJ)   65
Stirling Council, VAT Decision No. 17480   61
Stockton Plant & Equipment Ltd, VAT Decision No. 2093;
(1986) VATTR 94; (1986) 2 BVC 208,098   26
Stonecliff Caravan Park, VAT Decision No. 11097; [1994]
BVC 700   107
Strathearn Gordon Associates Ltd, VAT Decision
No. 1844; (1985) VATTR 79; (1985) 2 BVC 208,069   11
Stuttard (t/a De Wynns Coffee House), VAT Decision
No. 15982; [1999] BVC 4,074   51

Talacre Beech Caravans Sales Ltd v C & E Commrs [2004]
EWHC 165 (Ch); [2004] BVC 538   25
Tameside Metropolitan Borough Council (1979)
VATTR 93; (1979) 1 BVC 1,103   68
Temple House Developments Ltd, VAT Decision
No. 15583; [1998] BVC 2,302   115
Tobell, VAT Decision No. 16646; [2000] BVC 4,111   116
Tolsma v Inspecteur der Omzetbelasting Leeuwarden
(Case C-16/93) [1994] ECR I-743; [1994] BVC 117
(ECJ)   7
Tower Hamlets Housing Action Trust, VAT Decision
No. 17308; [2001] BVC 4,163   98
Trade Only Plant Sales Ltd, VAT Decision No. 18847;
[2005] BVC 4,041 . . . .   71, 102
Tremerton v C & E Commrs [2000] BVC 3; [1999]
STC 1039   38
Trewby v C & E Commrs [1976] 2 All ER 199; (1976)
1 BVC 80; [1976] STC 122   67
Trident Housing Association Ltd, VAT Decision
No. 10642; [1994] BVC 1,331   110

UFD Ltd, VAT Decision No. 1172; (1981) VATTR 199;
(1981) 1 BVC 1,164   72

Ultimate Advisory Services Ltd, VAT Decision No. 9523;
[1993] BVC 743; [1993] STI 345   69
Union of Students of the University of Warwick [1995]
V & DR 219; VAT Decision No. 13821; [1996]
BVC 4,236   145
United Biscuits (UK) Ltd v C & E Commrs [1992]
BVC 54; [1992] STC 325 (Ct of Sess)   23
University of Bath, VAT Decision No. 14235; [1996]
BVC 2,909   112
University of Hull, VAT Decision No. 180; (1984)
2 BVC 208,033   130
Uratemp Ventures Ltd v Collins [2002] 1 AC 301; [2001]
3 WLR 806 (HL)   112
Urdd Gobaith Cymru, VAT Decision No. 14881; [1997]
BVC 2,394   119

Van Boeckel v C & E Commrs (1980) 1 BVC 378   49
Van Tiem v Staatssecretararis van Financiën
(Case C-186/89) [1990] ECR I-4363; [1993] BVC 52
(ECJ)   17
Verbond van Nederlandse Ondernemingen v Inspecteur
der Invoerrechten en Accijnzen (Case 51/76) [1977]
ECR 113; [1977] 1 CMLR 413 (ECJ)   43
Vincett, VAT Decision No. 10932; [1994] BVC 1,401   151

Wade, VAT Decision No. 13164; [1996] BVC 4,085   134
Wallis Ltd, VAT Decision No. 18012; [2003] BVC 4,087 . .   120
Walsingham College (Yorkshire Properties) Ltd,
VAT Decision No. 13223; [1996] BVC 2,240   141
Watson, VAT Decision No. 18675; [2004] BVC 4,111   152
Watters, VAT Decision No. 13337; [1996] BVC 2,361   87
Wellcome Trust, VAT Decision No. 18417; [2004]
BVC 2,072   148
Wells, VAT Decision No. 15169; [1998] BVC 4,016   139
Wendy Fair Market Club, VAT Decision No. 679   68
West Devon District Council v C & E Commrs [2001]
BVC 525; [2001] STC 1282 (ChD)   61
West Lothian College SPV Ltd, VAT Decision No. 18133;
[2003] BVC 4,117   41
WH Payne & Co, VAT Decision No. 13668; [1996]
BVC 2,551   27
Whitbread Harrowden Settlement (Trustees of)
(and related appeals), VAT Decision No. 16781; [2001]
BVC 4,036   43

Table of Cases

White, VAT Decision No. 15338; [1998] BVC 2,167   87
Whitehead, VAT Decision No. 202; (1975) VATTR 152 . .   19
Williamson, VAT Decision No. 555; (1978) VATTR 90 . . .   52
Wilson, VAT Decision No. 428   79
Window, VAT Decision No. 17186; [2001] BVC 2,299 . . .   24
Winterthur Life UK Ltd, VAT Decision No. 15785; [1999]
    BVC 2,093
Wiseman, VAT Decision No. 17374; [2001] BVC 4,182 . . .   90
Wolverhampton and Dudley Breweries plc,
    VAT Decision No. 5351; (1990) VATTR 131; (1990)
    5 BVC 860   68
Woodley Baptist Church, VAT Decision No. 17833;
    VAT Decision No. 4,043   124
Wynn Realisations Ltd v Vogue Holdings Inc [1999]
    BVC 245; [1999] STC 524 (CA) 33, 71

Zanex Ltd, VAT Decision No. 17460; [2002] BVC 4,023 . .   21
Zita Modes Sàrl v Administration de l'enregistrement
    et des domaines (Case C-497/01) [2003] ECR I-14393;
    [2003] All ER (D) 411 (Nov)   101

1
General principles

1.1 WHAT IS VAT?

Value added tax ('VAT') is a tax charged on the supply of goods and services by businesses in the United Kingdom ('UK'). Unlike income tax or corporation tax, it is not related to business profits – it is a tax on consumption with the cost falling on the final consumer.

VAT has its origins in European legislation and was introduced in the UK on 1 April 1973 as a result of the government joining the European Community. The aim of the legislation is to create a common system of taxation that does not impede intra European Union ('EU') business transactions.

1.2 THE LEGISLATION

The main legislative provisions are contained in both European and national law.

First Council Directive of the European Union (77/227/EEC) ('First VAT Directive')
This directive defines the principles of VAT for application throughout the European Community.

Second Council Directive of the European Union (67/227/EEC) ('Second VAT Directive')
This directive set out the process of establishing VAT systems in member states. It was withdrawn and replaced by the Sixth VAT Directive in May 1977.

Sixth Council Directive of the European Union (77/388/EEC) ('Sixth VAT Directive')
This directive replaces the Second VAT Directive and further clarifies and details the treatment of transactions for VAT purposes throughout the European Community.

These directives are an important point of reference for VAT and take precedence over national law in member states. The European Court of Justice ('ECJ') often provides opinions on VAT matters referred from member states.

Value Added Tax Act 1994 ('VAT Act 1994')
This is the main UK legislation as amended by and expanded upon by subsequent finance bills and numerous statutory instruments. The Act is under the care and management of HM Revenue & Customs (the newly integrated tax authority formed from a merger of HM Customs & Excise and the Inland Revenue – referred to as 'Customs' in this text).

Value Added Tax Regulations 1995, (SI 1995/2518) ('VAT Regulations 1995')
These regulations set out the procedural details of aspects of the VAT Act 1994 including matters such as invoicing, VAT returns, time of supply, tax points and mechanisms for VAT recovery in particular instances.

1.2.1 Application of European law

Becker v Finanzamt Munster-Innenstadt (1981)

Where the provisions of a European Directive appear to be unconditional and sufficiently precise, these provisions may be relied upon by an individual against the state, to the extent that legislation in the member state concerned is incompatible with the Directive.

EC Commission v United Kingdom (1985)

The UK was ruled to have contravened the provisions of the Sixth VAT Directive by zero-rating (amongst other supplies) certain supplies of construction services in connection with commercial property. The Sixth Directive only permits the retention of zero rates where they are for clearly defined social reasons and for the benefit of the final consumer.

1.3 THE BASIC OPERATION OF VAT

The basic principle of VAT is that it is intended to be a tax on consumption and borne by the final consumer.

In general, VAT is charged at each stage of the production and distribution process in the course of providing goods or services, with the total tax due falling to the final consumer. Each business in this process is accountable to Customs for its VAT affairs.

1.3.1 Output tax

When a business makes a supply on which VAT is due, the VAT element is known as 'output tax'. This 'output tax' is passed onto Customs periodically by way of VAT returns.

1.3.2 Input tax

When a business pays for a purchase to be used for the purposes of their business, the VAT element is known as 'input tax'. This 'input tax' can be deducted from the 'output tax' above in calculating how much VAT is actually paid to Customs. If this purchase does not relate to a taxable supply by the business, the VAT component is not 'input tax' and may not be recovered.

The final consumer makes no supplies himself. He collects no output tax and so has nothing against which the VAT which he has paid out can be credited.

1.3.3 The VAT return

Value added tax is accounted for by a system of prescribed accounting periods and VAT returns. These returns are generally made quarterly, although different trader circumstances may allow or dictate a monthly or annual return. The excess of VAT collected from customers over VAT paid out on purchases is passed to Customs. The completed

VAT return and any payment due must be received by Customs within one month of the end of the prescribed accounting period.

1.3.4 Restrictions on VAT recovery

Some supplies do not give rise to the requirement to account to Customs for VAT either because they are non-business or they are specifically classed as exempt from VAT (to be distinguished from zero-rated). If a business makes exempt or non-business supplies then VAT recovery on cost components of the supply will be restricted.

1.4 THE MAIN VAT CHARGING PROVISION

The main VAT charging provision in the UK is found in the VAT Act 1994. The various terms that form this provision are elaborated upon in the following sections.

VAT Act 1994, section 4(1)

'VAT shall be charged on any supply of goods or services made in the United Kingdom, where it is a taxable supply made by a taxable person in the course or furtherance of any business carried on by him.'

Crown copyright material is reproduced with the permission of the Controller of HMSO and the Queen's Printer for Scotland.

This UK provision is derived from the Sixth VAT Directive which states that the supply of goods or services for a consideration by a taxable person shall be subject to VAT. The importation of goods will also be subject to VAT.

For any transaction, a multitude of factors must be considered in order to determine its VAT treatment. This will include establishing characteristics such as: is there a supply at all; if there is a supply, is VAT due; if VAT is due, at what rate; is it VAT-exempt; is it outside the scope of VAT; is it a supply of goods or services; what is the value of the supply; when and where is it made; who is the recipient of the supply and who pays for it?

1.5 THE CONCEPT OF SUPPLY

The concept of a supply is fundamental to the operation of the VAT system. The scope of the term 'supply' is intentionally very wide, and aims to include most normal commercial transactions. This includes sale, hire or lease of goods, supplies of services and also the waiving of certain contractual rights.

The basic definition of a supply is set out below:

VAT Act 1994, section 5(2)

'(a) "supply" in this Act includes all forms of supply, but not anything done otherwise than for a consideration;

(b) anything which is not a supply of goods but is done for a consideration (including, if so done, the granting, assignment or surrender of any right) is a supply of services.'

Crown copyright material is reproduced with the permission of the Controller of HMSO and the Queen's Printer for Scotland.

Transactions that fail to meet the above criteria will not be 'supplies' for VAT purposes unless they are deemed supplies (VAT Act 1994, Schedule 4).

1.5.1 Cases where held that a supply was made

Carlton Lodge Club v C & E Commrs (1974)

It was held that a supply arises where there is a transaction between two parties, where one furnishes or serves, and the other receives.

Cheshire Chimneys (1990)

A company renovated some properties for a property investor who offered a profit share on sale of the property. VAT was not accounted for on this payment. The tribunal held that as the investor and company were not in partnership the payment was most likely to be for the supply of building services, and therefore a supply was made, and the company must account for VAT on the payment received.

R v Goodwin and Unstead (1997)

The supply of counterfeit perfume was held to be a supply for VAT purposes as there was likely to be a degree of competition between the sale of counterfeit perfumes and that of genuine ones.

Keydon Estates Ltd (1990)

It was held that a profit sharing agreement did not amount to a partnership and therefore, a supply of services had arisen. Customs were therefore entitled to raise an assessment for the VAT in connection with a supply of services upon which VAT would be due.

1.5.2 Cases where held that no supply was made

Mol v Inspecteur der Invoerrechten en Accijnzen (1986)

The illegal supply of drugs was held not to be a supply for VAT purposes. In contrast with *R v Goodwin and Unstead* (1997) above, there was a total prohibition on the circulation of such products and therefore, there could be no element of competition between possible legitimate economic activities and this unlawful activity.

J Hopkins (Contractors) Ltd (1989)

A civil engineering company engaged labour-only subcontractors to carry out specific work. All materials were invoiced to and paid for by the company. Customs issued an assessment on the basis that the arrangements constituted a supply by the contractor to the subcontractor of the materials and plant hire, at cost, and a composite supply of goods and services back to the contractor by the subcontractor of the completed works. The tribunal allowed the company's appeal, holding that the materials were the sole responsibility of the main contractor from start to finish and therefore, no supply had taken place.

Iliffe (1993)

Where a landlord agrees to meet the additional cost to a tenant of an interest rate rise, the resulting payment is not seen as being consideration for any supply by the tenant. The payment was part and parcel of the original leasing agreement.

Tolsma v Inspecteur der Omzetbelasting Leeuwarden (1993)

In order for there to be a supply of services, there must be a direct link between the service and any payment received. A busker on the street who received donations from the public was held by the ECJ not to be supplying services for a consideration. Therefore, he was not required to account for VAT on the money received.

Church Schools Foundation Ltd v C & E Commrs (2001)

It was held in the Court of Appeal that a payment of £1m between two charities was a donation received without obligation and was therefore outside the scope of VAT. Customs had contended that VAT was due on the payment as it related to property maintenance works carried out on school buildings. As there was no direct link between the donation and the building work, the payment did not represent consideration for supplies of services.

KapHag Renditefonds 35 Spreecenter Berlin-Hellersdorf 3 Tanche GbR v Finanzamt Charlottenburg (2001)

A partner was admitted into an existing partnership on payment of a sum of money. The partnership reclaimed input tax on legal fees relating to this. The tax authority rejected the claim on the basis that the fees related to an exempt supply of allowing the new partner to take an active part in the partnership's business. The ECJ ruled that the entry of a new partner into a partnership in consideration for a contribution in cash was not to be regarded as an economic activity and therefore, the admission did not constitute a supply of services.

Kretztechnik AG v Finanzamt Linz (2003)

Kretztechnik sought to recover VAT incurred on costs associated with a listing on the German stock exchange. The German tax authorities denied VAT recovery on the basis that the issue of shares is an exempt activity for VAT purposes. The Advocate General said that the issue of new shares by a company in relation to a listing on the stock exchange is not a supply for VAT purposes and that VAT incurred by the company on costs relating to the issue should be treated as residual VAT. The full ECJ decision is awaited. This opinion is contrary to Customs' long-held policy that no VAT is recoverable in such instances.

1.5.3 Cases regarding deemed supplies

DCM Leisure Ltd (2000)

A company had purchased some land and recovered VAT paid to the vendor. The company failed to make any subsequent supplies and was later deregistered. Customs issued an assessment charging VAT on the basis that the value of the land had increased. The company appealed, contending that the land was almost worthless and therefore the VAT due should be negligible. The tribunal rejected this contention and dismissed the appeal, holding that the assessment had been made to the best of Customs' judgment.

Broadhurst (t/a RMS Heating) (1985)

A married couple who traded as central heating engineers carried out work on their own house. The work was invoiced to the husband and the necessary materials were purchased by the partnership. They did not account for

VAT on this invoice. The tribunal dismissed the couple's appeal holding that Customs' assessment was correct on the basis that there had been a deemed supply of materials.

1.5.4 Deemed non-supplies

Payments to staff

The VAT legislation excludes employees from the requirement to account for VAT on any services they provide to their employer in the course of carrying out their duties as employees.

VAT groups

Where two or more bodies corporate are registered as a VAT group, any supply of goods or services by one member of the group to another member of the group is disregarded for the purposes of VAT.

Transfer of going concern

Subject to specific rules the sale of the assets of a business will be treated as outside the scope of VAT, where a business or part of a business is transferred as a going concern.

1.5.5 Consideration

Consideration in the simplest of transactions can consist of money. However, consideration includes anything capable of being expressed in monetary terms including barter transactions and part exchanges. For VAT purposes, the consideration must be directly linked to the making of a supply.

In most transactions, the consideration is taken to be the VAT-inclusive value of the supply. The VAT value is determined by taking 7/47ths of the consideration for a standard-rated supply at 17.5%, or 1/21ths for a 5% reduced-rate supply.

Staatssecretaris van Financiën v Coöperatieve Aardappelenbewaarplaats GA (1980)

The court stated that the expression 'consideration' means everything received in return for a supply. This includes the value of any goods received in exchange for the supply.

Keeping Newcastle Warm v C & E Commrs (2000)

A network installer received government grants in respect of energy advice it gave to householders. It claimed a refund of the VAT it had paid on these payments on the basis that the grants were not consideration for any supplies. The ECJ held that the VAT legislation intended that VAT was due on subsidies received.

Land exchange deals

Cumbernauld Development Corporation (1992)

A development corporation exchanged some land with a golf club. No money changed hands although the development corporation had to carry out substantial works on the golf club's buildings. There was a dispute on the value on which VAT was to be charged. The tribunal held that in valuing the consideration its value had to be 'calculated subjectively by determining the value attributed by Cumbernauld Development Corporation to what they obtained'.

Ridgeons Bulk Ltd v C & E Commrs (1994)

A tenant agreed a rent-free period with a landlord in exchange for which the tenant was required to carry out repairs and refurbishment works to a building. It was held that the rent-free period amounted to consideration for a taxable supply. The tenant was therefore obliged to account for output tax on the repairs supplied to the landlord.

1.6 PROFIT SHARING AGREEMENTS, PARTNERSHIPS AND JOINT VENTURES

It is not uncommon that the parties to property development may enter in a profit sharing arrangement based on the end value of the development. The VAT treatment of such arrangements can lead to unexpected VAT charges.

Strathearn Gordon Associates Ltd (1985)

A management consultancy business received a specified percentage of the total profits in respect of a property development. It argued that it did not have to account for VAT on this payment as the payment was the result of a joint venture agreement which amounted to a partnership – supplies between partners being outside the scope of VAT. It was held that the essential requirements of a partnership were not fulfilled and that the company had agreed to supervise the work carried out and this was a taxable supply of services.

Fivegrange Ltd (1989)

A company carried on the business of property development entered into a joint venture agreement with another company under which it was to receive a fixed fee plus a percentage of any profits of the venture. No VAT was accounted for and Customs issued an assessment. Fivegrange contended that the agreement amounted to a partnership. The tribunal held that the agreement did not amount to a partnership.

C & E Commrs v Latchmere Properties Ltd (2005)

A company owned some properties which it wished to redevelop and sell. A development agreement was entered into with Latchmere. Latchmere received part of the sale proceeds. No VAT was accounted for and Customs issued an assessment on the basis that payment was for standard-rated construction services. Latchmere contended that it had acquired an interest in the land under the agreement and the payment from the property-owning company to them was a receipt in connection with the sale of VAT-exempt land. The tribunal held that the agreement amounted to a joint venture rather than a simple supply of construction services and therefore no VAT was due.

Bird Semple & Crawford Herron (1986)

It was confirmed that supplies to a nominee company, which held a lease for a partnership, were really supplies made to the partnership as beneficial owners.

1.7   GOODS AND SERVICES

A supply can be classed as the transfer of ownership of goods or the provision of services. The VAT Act 1994, Schedule 4 identifies supplies which, for clarity, are defined in the legislation to be either goods or services, e.g. supplies of electricity are goods or the grant of a short lease (less than 21 years in England) is a supply of services.

1.7.1   Goods

A supply of goods is made when exclusive ownership of goods is passed to another person. Items that are deemed to be goods for VAT purposes include the grant of 'a major interest in land'.

A 'major interest in land' is the sale of a freehold, or the grant or assignment of a lease exceeding 21 years under English law. In Scotland the equivalent of a freehold sale is the sale of the estate or interest of the owner. For leases in Scotland, a major interest is a lease of not less than 20 years.

C & E Commrs v Oliver (1980)

A 'supply' has been interpreted as meaning the passing of possession in goods pursuant to an agreement, whereby the supplier agrees to part and the recipient agrees to take possession. 'Possession' has been taken to mean control over the goods, in order that the recipient will have immediate facility for their use.

Seaton Parochial Church Council (2004)

It was held that where a church had bought heaters to be installed in a listed church that this was a supply of goods and only capable of being treated as VAT standard-rated at 17.5%. The services of the separate contractor who installed the heaters were zero-rated as approved alterations to a protected building.

1.7.2 Services

A supply of services arises when something is done, other than supplying goods, in return for 'consideration'. This includes other interests in land, such as the supply of a lease of less than 21 years.

Richards (1986)

It was held that a payment to an architect in relation to an abandoned project was not compensation but consideration for a supply of services on which VAT was due.

Shingler Risdon Associates (1988)

A property developer who could not guarantee a development project was going to go ahead made a payment described as an 'interest-free loan' to a firm of architects who were drawing up the scheme. No VAT was accounted for on the loan. The loan was to be repaid if the project proceeded and the architect's fees paid accordingly.

The project was aborted and the 'loan' was not repaid. The tribunal dismissed the firm's appeal, holding that the payment was consideration for the services which the firm had supplied and VAT was due.

22a Property Investments Ltd (1996)

Following a collapsed land deal, a property company assigned the right to share in the proceeds of litigation with another company. This assignment was held to be a taxable supply of services and payments received were consideration for that supply. The recipient of the payments was therefore entitled to register for VAT.

1.8   TAXABLE SUPPLIES

A taxable supply means a business supply that is defined as taxable in that VAT must be charged on that supply at either the standard rate of 17.5%, the reduced rate of 5% or the zero rate of VAT. The rate of VAT will depend on the nature of the taxable supply being made.

In addition to taxable supplies, there are other supplies which are either VAT-exempt or outside the scope of VAT.

Whether a supply is (1) taxable, (2) exempt, or (3) outside the scope of VAT will be dictated by the detail of the VAT legislation and the associated case law, and in turn, this classification will determine liability to register for VAT, how much VAT on sales (output tax) is accounted for to Customs, and how much VAT on purchases (input tax) that suppliers can recover in connection with their onward supplies.

C & E Commrs v Briararch Ltd (1992)

Briararch carried out work to a building with the intention of granting a 25-year zero-rated lease enabling full VAT recovery. However, due to market conditions, they granted a 4-year lease which was exempt from VAT thus debarring VAT recovery. It was determined by the court that Briararch could recover 25/29ths of the input tax as they had retained the intention of granting the zero-rated long lease.

Isaac (1996)

The grant of leases of newly built residential apartments in excess of 21 years is a taxable supply giving the right to recover VAT on related construction costs. Where leases where granted for terms not exceeding 21 years, an exempt supply would result with no VAT recovery being allowed. It was accepted that a deed of rectification to extend the short leases to make taxable supplies and thus secure VAT recovery was valid where a genuine mistake had been made.

1.9 TAXABLE PERSON

1.9.1 'Taxable person' – UK and European definitions

The UK legislation states a 'taxable person' is an individual, partnership or company who is, or is required to be, registered for VAT.

European legislation defines a 'taxable person' as any person who independently carries out in any place any economic activity whatever the purpose or results of that activity. This excludes employed and other persons from the tax in so far as they are bound to an employer by contracts of employment or by any other legal ties creating the relationship of employer and employee as regards working conditions, remuneration and the employer's liability (Sixth VAT Directive, Article 4).

1.9.1.1 UK perspective – business

The UK VAT legislation states that a business includes any trade, profession or vocation. There are also activities which are deemed businesses for VAT purposes including the provision by a club, association or organisation of the facilities or advantages available to its members; and the admission for a consideration of persons to any premises.

1.9.1.2 European perspective – economic activity

The European legislation uses the term 'economic activity' which is deemed to include all activities of producers, traders and persons supplying services including mining and agricultural activities, and activities of the professions. The exploitation of tangible or intangible property for the purposes of obtaining income on a continuing basis is also considered an economic activity.

Occasional transactions are also confirmed as being economic activities including, in particular, the supply before first occupation of buildings or parts of buildings and the land on which they stand, and the supply of building land.

Staatssecretaris van Financiën v Heerma (1998)

Where a person's sole economic activity consisted of the letting of a large shed to a farming company or partnership of which he was a member, the letting was to be regarded as an independent economic activity within the meaning of Article 4(1) of the Sixth VAT Directive.

1.9.2 Case law

1.9.2.1 Business

C & E Commrs v Morrison's Academy Boarding Houses Association (1978)

This case concerned a private school recognised as a charity. The school argued that, as a charity, it was not a business. However, it was held that a charity could be in business, as supplies could be made for a consideration. It was held that profit was not a necessity in order to have a business.

Van Tiem v Staatssecretaris van Financiën (1989)

The grant of a right over immoveable property for 18 years for an annual payment was an economic activity for VAT purposes. The expression 'economic activity' stems from Article 4(1) of the Sixth VAT Directive and is wider than the term 'business' used in the UK legislation.

Williamson (1978)

The letting of garages was held to be a business as the taxpayers were actively involved in the management of the garages and letting them to tenants and not only passively receiving rents.

1.9.2.2 **Non-business**

C & E Commrs v Lord Fisher (1981)

Lord Fisher ran shooting parties for his friends as a hobby. Customs contended that he was in business and should account for VAT on the payments he received to fund the shoots. However, he was held not to have been in business, based on consideration of a number of factors, including the level of commerciality, the continuity of operations, the creation of an entity distinct from its separate parts, the element of organisation, the question of whether the shoots were a 'serious undertaking earnestly pursued', were carried on for some form of payment; and were not being carried out for pleasure or as a hobby.

National Society for the Prevention of Cruelty to Children (1993)

The mere investment of money and the sale and purchase of investments did not constitute a business even though professionally managed and carried out on a large scale.

Archer (1974)

A house built on land for one's own occupation will not give rise to a business activity and VAT registration will not be allowed.

Mellerstain Trust (Trustees of) (1989)

It was held that pictures acquired as a gift and subsequently sold by the Trust were not done so in the course of any business for VAT purposes. VAT could only be charged if the assets were used in the furtherance of a business. There was no evidence that a business was being carried on.

The sale of the paintings was also a disposal of capital items for VAT purposes. The disposal of such items is specifically excluded from being included in the value of a person's supplies for determining whether VAT registration is required (VAT Act 1994, Schedule A1, paragraph 1(7)).

Sawyer (2003)

A man who registered for and recovered VAT on the refurbishment of his own listed house was considered not to be in business as he made no supplies of building services to anyone.

Finanzamt Uelzen v Armbrecht (1992)

A hotelier sold a guesthouse, part of which he had used for private purposes rather than for business purposes. It was held that where a taxable person sold property, part of which he had chosen to reserve for private use, the sale of that part was outside the scope of VAT.

1.9.3 Registration

1.9.3.1 Compulsory registration

Registration for VAT is compulsory if a taxable person makes taxable supplies in excess of the registration threshold. The threshold for 2005/06 is £60,000, effective from 1 April 2005. Registration is the only way for a business established in the UK to recover input tax on its expenditure.

Whitehead (1975)

A woman was late notifying Customs of her liability to register. It was held that Customs were obliged to backdate her registration and had no discretion to waive the statutory provisions.

1.9.3.2 **Voluntary registration**

A person has the right to register for VAT even if the value of taxable supplies does not reach the registration threshold, thus allowing for the recovery of VAT incurred in making those taxable supplies (providing that the person is in business).

1.9.3.3 **Intending trader**

Registration is also allowed on an 'intending trader' basis. This is relevant for those who have the intention to make taxable supplies of land, and wish to recover VAT on costs prior to making any supplies.

Hordern (1992)

A business registered and recovered VAT. Customs tried to reclaim VAT from the business as it never made any taxable supplies. Custom's action was held to be in contravention of the Sixth VAT Directive as there was a genuine intention to make supplies.

Rompelman & another v Minister van Financiën (1983)

It was held that VAT can be reclaimed on a 'statement of intention' that a taxable supply would be made. Objective evidence may be required to support the claim. In this case, the property owner sought to register and recover VAT on the basis that they intended to let a property. It was held that there was an economic activity and the taxpayer was entitled to register for, and recover, VAT.

Intercommunale voor Zeewaterontzilting (INZO) v Belgian State (1994)

As long as a business always had the intention to make taxable supplies there is no right for Customs to demand repayment of VAT recovered by a business in the event that that business fails.

1.9.3.4 Pre-registration VAT

VAT incurred on goods and services prior to registration may be recovered, subject to specific conditions. Evidence must be retained and the VAT must be recovered in the first VAT return. VAT on goods is recoverable up to three years before registration and up to six months prior to registration on services.

Elliot (1990)

The tribunal held that VAT on services supplied more than six months before registration was not recoverable. Building services could not be split into component supplies of goods and services, thereby allowing the three-year rule to apply to the goods.

Park Avenue Methodist Church (Trustees of) (2001)

The Trustees completed building works and incurred VAT. Somewhat later they applied to register for VAT and made the option to tax. The construction services were outside the six-month limit and VAT recovery was not permitted under the legislation. It was held that it would be wholly artificial to separate construction goods from a supply of construction services for the purposes of benefiting from the three-year pre-registration rules for VAT on goods.

1.9.4 Deregistration

Zanex Ltd (2001)

A company purchased a property for £520,000 plus VAT of £91,000. It registered for VAT in February 1995, stating on form VAT1 that it was carrying on a business of property letting. In its first return, it reclaimed the VAT as input tax. However, it never accounted for any output tax, and in July 1997 it applied for its registration to be cancelled. Customs accepted the application and issued an assessment charging VAT of £99,842 on the deemed value of the property. The tribunal upheld the assessment and dismissed the company's appeal.

1.9.5 VAT groups

A number of associated businesses can apply to Customs to be treated as a VAT group. There are specific rules as to the nature of association required and Customs have powers to refuse an application if they suspect there are VAT avoidance motives.

The principal effects of grouping are that transactions between group members can be disregarded for VAT purposes and a representative member completes a single VAT return for the group.

This leads to advantages such as simplified administration, scope for increased VAT recovery if a VAT-exempt company is involved and less risk of misdeclaration penalties.

There are complicated anti-avoidance rules to deal with corporate structures which seek to take advantage of VAT grouping to reduce tax costs.

C & E Commrs v Kingfisher (1994)

A VAT group is treated as if it were a single taxable person, even though the group will be taxable through a single representative member of that group.

National Westminster Bank plc (1998)

Customs have said they will refuse to allow a company to join a group where they are not satisfied that the VAT savings arise as a natural result of grouping. In this case, they will use revenue protection powers to prevent the perceived VAT avoidance taking place.

C & E Commrs v Barclays Bank plc (2001)

The members of a VAT group are joint and severally liable for the VAT debts of their fellow members.

1.10 MULTIPLE OR COMPOUND SUPPLIES

Where a number of different goods or services are sold together, an issue may arise as to the VAT treatment of the items supplied. The VAT treatment could vary depending on whether the goods or services are treated together or separately.

The two options are:

(1) a multiple supply (this arises where the different elements are treated separately for VAT purposes); or

(2) a composite supply (which arises where all the component parts are treated as having a single VAT liability, based on the liability of the principal item of supply).

1.10.1 The current test

Card Protection Plan Ltd v C & E Commrs (1996)

This case related to the VAT liability of two services provided by Card Protection Plan Ltd – insurance services and card registration services following the loss of credit cards by customers. The courts held that the principal feature of the supply was the insurance element, and it was therefore a composite VAT exempt supply of insurance services.

The European Court of Justice (ECJ) stated that in order to distinguish between multiple and composite supplies, the perception of the purchaser must be identified. If, for instance, the customer thought that two things were being supplied and that both were important, then there would be a multiple supply. On the other hand, if one supply was ancillary or incidental to the other, then there was likely to be a single compound supply. A supply could be regarded as ancillary to the principal service if it did not constitute an aim in itself, but only a means of better enjoying the principal supply made.

1.10.2 Composite supplies

United Biscuits (UK) Ltd v C & E Commrs (1992)

It was held that a biscuit tin containing biscuits was a single zero-rated supply of biscuits. The tin was incidental to, or an integral part of, the supply of biscuits.

Richard Haynes Associates (1992)

Where a flat is let and additionally laundry, shopping and secretarial services are provided, these were held in this case to be incidental to the exempt rental income and thus no VAT recovery was permitted.

First Base Properties Ltd (1993)

The landlord charged separately for rental of office space and for various services (telephone, fax, copying, use of furniture). It was held there were two separate supplies.

Clowance Holdings Ltd (2001)

In a case regarding charges for management and maintenance to timeshare owners, the tribunal considered whether such payments were part of the original timeshare lease and therefore taxed on the basis of the lease. It was held that they were not and that payments were taxable in their own right.

Blendhome Ltd t/a Stanhill Court Hotel (1999)

The tribunal held there was a single standard-rated supply of hotel accommodation for the purpose of catering at a wedding with associated accommodation provided, and not an exempt licence to occupy.

Window (2000)

The appellant was held to be making a single exempt supply of the right to occupy a stable and not two supplies – (1) of exempt stabling, and (2) of VAT standard-rated livery services.

1.10.3 Multiple supplies

Rayner & Keeler Ltd v C & E Commrs (1994)

This case was concerned with the VAT liability of shopfitting contracts for a retail optician. The High Court held that the shopfitting contracts under each section of the contract involved a substantial and complex commercial relationship and in substance and reality comprised multiple separable supplies of goods and multiple separable supplies of services. The tribunal had erred in law in concluding that the supplies in every section were integral components of a single supply of shopfitting services. The matter was remitted to the tribunal to consider and analyse the individual supplies to determine whether each supply of goods was an integral part of a supply of services or vice versa.

C & E Commrs v Jeffs (t/a J & J Joinery) (1995)

In this case, the judge made it clear that a composite supply of goods, with the services being incidental, would apply only where the services involved merely constituted satisfaction of the seller's obligations imposed by law.

Burgess (t/a Cards n Cuddles) (1996)

This case was also concerned with whether a shopfitting contract was a single supply of services or a mixed supply of goods and services. It was held that there was a composite supply of services, the goods being incidental.

Softley Ltd (t/a Softley Kitchens) (1996)

In contrast, the supply of a fitted kitchen was held to be a composite supply of goods, with the fitting services being incidental to that supply.

Talacre Beech Caravans Sales Ltd v C & E Commrs (2004)

A company sold some caravans and accounted for VAT on the removable contents (cooking appliances, furniture, curtains and carpets). Subsequently, the company requested a repayment of VAT on the basis of the *Card Protection Plan* decision arguing that there was a single zero-rated supply. The courts disagreed with the company holding that the legislation specifically prevented these items from being zero-rated.

1.11 ARE THE SUPPLIES 'MADE IN THE UK'?

1.11.1 Supplies of goods

A supply of goods takes place in the UK if the goods are in the UK at the time they are supplied. A supply of goods which are removed from the UK is still 'made in the UK' but is likely to be VAT zero-rated as a dispatch or export.

If goods are brought into the UK from overseas, there will be a liability for the supplier if they are supplying the goods in the UK, or for the purchaser if they are acquiring goods from the EU or importing goods from outside the EU. Customs will usually collect VAT at the point of entry into the UK.

A supply of goods which are not in the UK carries no UK VAT liability or registration (although it may lead to a requirement to register in the country concerned).

There are special rules for installed goods. Installed goods are taken as being supplied at the place of installation. This will probably require a UK VAT registration for an overseas trader installing goods in the UK. If this is a one-off contract for the overseas supplier, and the supply is to a VAT-registered customer, then the overseas supplier need not register. The UK-based customer can account for the VAT as an acquisition or import.

Stockton Plant & Equipment Ltd (1986)

A company zero-rated a supply of goods to another company for export to Libya. It was held that Customs were entitled to raise an assessment for VAT because the company had not produced sufficient documentary proof of the export occurring.

Somerset Car Sales Ltd (1993)

A UK company which sold a van to a non-VAT-registered resident of the Republic of Ireland was required to account for VAT on the sale as the condition that the recipient of the goods be VAT-registered was not satisfied.

Centrax Ltd (1998)

A UK company which manufactured, repaired and maintained gas turbine generators transferred parts to a depot in Italy for installation at a premises of a client. Customs assessed the business on the basis a deemed supply had been made because the parts had not been supplied to a customer and the company were not registered for VAT in Italy. As a result of this case, Customs now accept that deliveries to 'own branches' in other member states where no VAT registration exists can be zero-rated as long as the member states' VAT-registration rules do not allow backdated registrations and there is no avoidance.

1.11.2 Supplies of services

As a basic rule, a supply of services takes place where the supplier has established his business. When services are connected to land, the supply is deemed to take place where the land is located. This includes the services of estate agents, construction professionals, architects, project managers and surveyors. Registration may be required in the country concerned.

If a non-UK business supplies services in the UK related to land and their customer is registered for VAT in the UK, then they do not have to register for UK VAT. The UK customer can account for the VAT in their accounts by way of a reverse charge mechanism.

A UK business supplying land-related services overseas may have to register for VAT in the country concerned. However, some countries operate the same system as the UK so that the customer in the country concerned deals with the VAT through their VAT return.

Brodrick Wright & Strong Ltd (1986)

The surveyor of a damaged jetty located in the UK but appointed by companies registered in Hong Kong and Bermuda did not account for VAT on the supplies. It was held that the services were related to the land so the service was provided in the UK and VAT was therefore applicable.

WH Payne & Co (1995)

It was held that accountancy and taxation services provided to overseas companies which owned and let properties in the UK were not liable to VAT. This was because the companies concerned had no 'fixed establishment' in the UK.

Aspen Advisory Services Ltd (1994)

A UK company which provided management services to two Channel Islands companies in respect of UK-based properties was required to account for VAT on its services. It was held that the accounting and bookkeeping services were land-related and therefore taxable in the UK.

McLean & Gibson (Engineers) Ltd (2001)

A South African company bought some second-hand plant from Scotland. The UK company arranged for the removal and shipping of the goods and treated the transaction as a zero-rated export. It was held that VAT was chargeable as the company had supplied services related to the land.

Mechanical Engineering Consultants Ltd (1993)

Services supplied to a Swiss company relating to the commissioning of an industrial waste incinerator in the UK were held to be services relating to land. VAT was therefore chargeable on the supply.

1.12   EIGHTH VAT DIRECTIVE REFUNDS

The Eighth VAT Directive provides a mechanism by which member states can claim a refund of VAT on business-related transactions they have made in member states other than those where they have a VAT registration.

1.13   THIRTEENTH VAT DIRECTIVE REFUNDS

The Thirteenth VAT Directive provides a similar mechanism to the Eighth Directive for non-EU businesses incurring expenditure in the EU.

1.14   TIME OF SUPPLY

The exact time of a supply for VAT purposes is known as the 'tax point' and is determined by a detailed set of rules. The importance of correctly identifying the tax point is that this determines the particular tax return in which the tax is passed to Customs and the return in which it is recovered on purchases.

The basic tax point for a supply of goods is when they are removed from the supplier to the purchaser. For a supply of services it is when the services are performed or completed.

The basic tax point is overridden where there is the receipt of payment or tax invoice before the basic tax point. It is also overridden if the tax invoice is issued up to 14 days after the basic tax point. The 14-day rule can be extended by application to Customs.

It is possible to have more than one tax point for a single supply, for example, where a deposit is paid then the balance paid on delivery.

Rampling (1986)

A builder received a cheque and banked it one month later to take advantage of a change in the VAT rate. It was held that payment only occurred when the builder presented the cheque to the bank.

Dormers Builders Ltd v C & E Commrs (1989)

In this case, the aim was to trigger a tax point before a change in the VAT rate. The builder received a cheque and paid it into an escrow account. The builder could only access the money once an architect's certificate had been issued confirming the work had been completed. The court held that this deposit into an escrow account amounted to payment as the payer's obligations had been met in full and the builder had the right to sue for the money.

The Clean Car Co Ltd (1991)

When a company reclaimed VAT based on an architect's certificate rather than the builder's invoice, Customs imposed a misdeclaration penalty. Because of health issues with the company's staff, the tribunal accepted that the circumstances leading to this event amounted to a reasonable excuse.

1.14.1 Construction services

Revised tax point rules apply to any services of construction, alteration, demolition, repair or maintenance of a building or civil engineering work where services are performed after 8 June 1999. Under these rules, construction services are treated as separately and successively supplied, at the earliest of:

- each time that a payment is received by the supplier; or

- each time that the supplier issues a VAT invoice.

The exception to this rule applies, broadly, if the building in question will be occupied by a person connected with a supplier of the services, who will use the building other than mainly for taxable purposes. Where this exception applies, the tax point is the day when the work is completed (unless the services were performed between 9 December 1997 and 9 June 1999, in which case the tax point falls 18 months after completion).

1.14.2 Retention payments

The VAT element of a retention payment in a construction contract is accounted for by a contractor on the earlier of:

- the actual payment of the retention; or

- the issue of a VAT invoice.

Mercantile Contracts Ltd (1988)

The tribunal held that the time of supply for some construction services of converting a building to flats was when the services were performed despite the fact that the builder had agreed not to be paid until five years later.

Greater World Association Trust (1989)

A charity sought to recover VAT on estate agency fees on the basis that the supply took place before a date when changes in the VAT legislation would have prevented recovery. The completion of the property sales took place after the said date. It was held that where services are performed over a period of time and there was one consideration for the services as a whole, then the time when services are performed must be when all the services to be supplied have been performed, i.e. on completion of the sales.

Cooke (1984)

On registering for VAT, an estate agent did not add VAT to the fees agreed prior to his registration. It was held that VAT was due, as the time of supply of his fees was the relevant property completion date, rather than the date of agreeing the fees.

1.15 VALUATION OF SUPPLIES

The value of a supply for VAT purposes is important, as it forms the basis for calculating the amount of VAT due.

The VAT-inclusive value of the supply is known as the 'consideration'. The VAT value is determined by taking 7/47ths of the consideration for a standard-rated supply at 17.5%, or 1/21ths for a 5% reduced-rate supply.

Most pricing documents state that the price is VAT-exclusive and that VAT must be added to give the total consideration for the supply. If VAT is not mentioned, it is deemed to be included in the price given.

VAT Act 1994, section 89

If a supply is made and no mention of VAT is made, then the consideration is deemed to be inclusive of VAT unless there is an agreement stating VAT should be added or the transaction occurs in an industry where it is a trade practice to add VAT onto the price quoted. Section 89 of the VAT Act 1994 specifically allows, in relation to a tenancy or lease, that VAT can be added on top of the monies otherwise chargeable as rent. This can only be overridden by specific contract clauses.

C & E Commrs v Battersea Leisure Ltd (1993)

A company sold Battersea Power Station for £1.5m and also agreed to pay £2.2m as a contribution to asbestos removal costs. It was held that the recipient of the contribution had made a VATable supply on which VAT would have to be accounted for.

Love v Norman Wright Builders Ltd (1994)

'The plain fact is that the parties omitted to take purchase tax into consideration at all, and the incidence of the tax must lie where it falls. The plaintiff is accountable for it ...'

Franks & Collingwood v Gates (1985)

The relationship between a supplier and HM Customs & Excise cannot be affected by the contractual relationship between a supplier and his customer. The contractual terms can only affect who is ultimately responsible for bearing the cost of the tax between the two parties. VAT is the liability of the person making a supply. Under a contract the supplier can shift the burden of the tax to the recipient of the supply as is common practice. It is still the supplier who is responsible under law to pay the VAT to Customs.

ES Poyser & Sons Ltd v Capital & Counties plc (1989)

A landlord agreed to make a contribution of £55,000 to a tenant's shopfitting costs. The court held that it could be implied that this meant the full £55,000 would be available for shop fitting and was a figure net of VAT. The tenant therefore successfully sued the landlord for the VAT.

Jaymarke Developments v Elinacre Ltd (in liquidation) (1992)

Some land was sold and the price was stated to be inclusive of VAT. As the sale was VAT-exempt, no VAT was chargeable. The purchaser claimed that the price should be reduced by the amount of VAT chargeable if the sale had been VAT standard-rated at 17.5%. It was held that the price would be VAT-inclusive if any VAT was payable, as none was payable the purchaser had no valid claim.

Hostgilt Ltd v Megahart (1999)

This case held that a clause in a contract stating that sums payable were exclusive of VAT was to have the effect that if VAT did become chargeable, it would have to be added on to the price agreed in the contract. Conversely, if VAT was not specifically mentioned, and was due, then the price would be VAT-inclusive.

Wynn Realisations Ltd v Vogue Holdings Inc (1999)

Wynn sold a property to Vogue where the contract held the price was exclusive of VAT. It was assumed that the sale was exempt from VAT. It was discovered later that the building was 'new' and therefore VAT was due at 17.5%. Wynn paid the VAT to Customs and sought to recover it from Vogue. The court found for Wynn saying that the words 'exclusive of VAT' meant that if VAT was payable then it could be added to the sale price.

1.15.1 Discounts

If any prompt payment discount is offered, it is assumed that this will be taken, and VAT is therefore calculated on the discounted figure. This also applies to quantity-related discounts.

1.15.2 Tax deductions

Where a contractor is required by law to make a deduction on account of income tax from a payment to a subcontractor who is not exempt from such deduction, the tax value for VAT purposes of the subcontractor's services is the gross amount charged by him before deduction is made.

Any deduction in respect of the Construction Industry Training Board Levy, which has been agreed by the subcontractor, can be deducted from the gross amount for the purpose of calculating the VAT due, and the value of the supply will be treated as reduced by any such levy.

1.16   INPUT TAX RECOVERY

There are four principal stages to establishing the amount of recoverable VAT for a VAT-registered business as follows:

(1) Identify and discard irrecoverable VAT incurred in carrying out non-business activities.

(2) Identify recoverable VAT incurred in carrying out taxable activities – known as 'input tax'. The First VAT Directive refers to the deduction of 'the amount of VAT borne directly by the various cost components of taxable supplies'.

(3) Identify the irrecoverable VAT incurred in carrying out exempt activities – known as 'exempt input tax'. In certain situations, the exempt input tax may be recoverable where its value is below the de minimis limits set in the legislation.

(4) VAT that cannot be directly attributed wholly to taxable or exempt supplies is termed as 'residual'. This VAT is apportioned between taxable and exempt supplies on the basis of an apportionment calculation.

In addition, it will be necessary to consider whether any of the VAT relates to 'blocked input tax' or whether the use of any assets upon which VAT has been recovered needs to be monitored over time under the Capital Goods Scheme.

Variations in the level of taxable use of such assets will lead to VAT adjustments.

If all the VAT incurred is related to an onward taxable supply it can be recovered in full provided there is a direct and immediate link between the purchase and the onward taxable supply.

BLP Group plc v C & E Commrs (1995)

The ECJ held that input tax was only deductible if the goods and services in question had a direct and immediate link with taxable transactions. VAT on professional fees incurred in relation to a disposal of shares in a subsidiary was not deductible since they related entirely to the making of an exempt disposal of shares and were not related to capital raising for the business as a whole and therefore residual as the taxpayer contended.

C & E Commrs v Redrow Group Ltd (1999)

The developer tried to reclaim VAT that it had paid out settling the estate agency fees of prospective purchasers of their new homes. The estate agency fees related to the disposal of the existing homes of the prospective purchasers. Customs argued that there was no direct and immediate link between the sale of the new house and the payment of a third party's estate agency fees.

It was held that Redrow had complete control over the estate agents and invoices were raised to Redrow. Therefore, a 'direct and immediate link' existed and the VAT was recoverable.

1.16.1   VAT incurred on non-business activities

VAT incurred on non-business activities is not recoverable.

Ian Flockton Developments Ltd v C & E Commrs (1987)

A yacht was purchased and VAT recovery sought. It was held that the yacht was acquired for the director's personal enjoyment and therefore was not a business transaction.

David Grey Homes & Gardens Ltd (1987)

VAT incurred in relation to the refurbishment of a barn could only be recovered to the extent that the barn was used for business purposes.

D Dyball & Son (1989)

A farming partnership restored a derelict cottage and reclaimed the VAT. The tribunal held that the VAT was reclaimable despite the partnership not committing to the precise use of the building in the future. The tribunal had consideration for the diversification of many farming businesses – the property may have been used as a residence for one of the directors or as a holiday let.

I/S Fini H v Skatteministeriet (2003)

It was held that a person who had ceased economic activity, but was required to continue paying rent because of a non-termination clause in a lease agreement, was allowed to recover VAT on the rents.

1.16.2 VAT incurred on taxable or exempt activities

VAT on purchases attributable to taxable supplies (i.e. supplies with VAT charged at 0%, 5% or 17.5%) is recoverable in full whereas VAT on purchases attributable to exempt onward supplies will not be recoverable.

Where there is a change in business intention, there is the possibility of a clawback or repayment of VAT under regulations 108 and 109 of the VAT Regulations 1995. If a taxpayer has recovered VAT on purchases on the basis that they intended the purchases to be used exclusively in making taxable supplies, and then that intention changed within six years from the period when the original taxable intention was formed, then VAT must be accounted for to Customs to the extent the goods are used for exempt supplies.

Where an exempt intention with no VAT recovery changes to a taxable onward supply, additional VAT recovery is possible.

C & E Commrs v Briararch Ltd (1992)

Briararch carried out work to a building with the intention of granting a 25-year zero-rated lease enabling full VAT recovery. However, due to market conditions, they granted a four-year lease which was exempt from VAT thus debarring VAT recovery. It was determined by the court that Briararch could recover 25/29ths of the input tax as they had retained the intention of granting the zero-rated long lease.

C & E Commrs v Curtis Henderson (1992)

A house intended for sale was let for a period of nine months prior to sale. It was held that the VAT recovery would have to be apportioned in a similar manner to that in *C & E Commrs v Briararch*.

Belgian State v Ghent Coal Terminal NV (1998)

A company reclaimed VAT in connection with some land. The company was required to dispose of the land by Ghent Council without ever having used it for the taxable purposes it had intended. The Belgian tax authorities sought to recover the VAT on the basis no taxable supplies had been made. The ECJ held that the right of deduction remained where circumstances beyond the control of the taxpayer meant no taxable supplies were possible.

Tremerton v C & E Commrs (1999)

A property developer purchased a property with the intention of redeveloping it to form residential apartments for sale. It incurred expenditure on planning consultants, engineers, etc. and reclaimed the VAT on the basis it was intending to make taxable supplies. However, they were unable to gain the necessary finance to develop the site so made an exempt disposal of the site. Customs assessed for repayment of the VAT previously recovered. The courts held that Customs were entitled to ask for the repayment.

Royal & Sun Alliance Group plc v C & E Commrs (2001)

A tenant occupied an opted building paying VAT on the rent – the tenant had not opted to tax the property themselves as it was originally intended for their own occupation. Later, part of the property was vacated as it was surplus to requirements, and eventually sublet – the tenant having now opted to tax the property themselves. It was held that the company could recover the VAT on the rental payments made to their landlord during the void period as this rent was a cost component of the taxable rents received from their new subtenant.

C & E Commrs v Wiggett Construction (2001)

Wiggett purchased land and was charged VAT. Wiggett recovered the VAT on the basis that they intended to make taxable supplies of new housing. Within six years of this intention being made, Wiggett made an exempt land supply to a housing association as well as concurrently entering into a development contract to carry out construction works on the land. It was held that the VAT recovery should be apportioned between taxable building services and exempt supplies of land.
[This decision has since been overturned by the *Southern Primary Housing Ltd* case.]

C & E Commrs v Southern Primary Housing Ltd (2004)

A company purchased some land and was charged VAT. The intention was to obtain planning permission for residential development and sell the land to a housing association. The company made a VAT-exempt disposal of the land to the housing association, and also entered into a contract to construct the residential accommodation for the association. The company sought to recover an element of VAT on their land purchase as partly attributable to the taxable supply of construction work. It was held that no VAT recovery was possible as the land purchase was not a 'cost component' of the construction works.

Buckley (t/a Wheelcraft Centre & Original Homes) (1990)

It was held that VAT incurred on the refurbishment of an old pottery was to be attributed between the property owner's fully taxable antiques business and exempt short-term tenancies in respect of several workshops. Only VAT attributed to the taxable antiques business was recoverable.

Beaverbank Properties Ltd (2003)

A property development company incurred speculative costs in relation to a site it was interested in acquiring. Due to planning difficulties it had to abandon the site. It was held that the company was entitled to recover VAT as it was always the intention to opt to tax the site and make taxable supplies.

1.16.3 Partial exemption

Where a business incurs VAT on costs that is attributable to both taxable and exempt supplies, not all VAT paid out on purchases will be recoverable. A business of this type is known as 'partially exempt'. There are many partially exempt businesses, including those in the financial, health, welfare, education and property sectors.

After the direct attribution of VAT incurred on purchases to either taxable or exempt supplies, the remaining residual VAT on business overheads and the like needs to be appropriately apportioned. The method of making this apportionment needs to be agreed with Customs, with the exception of the standard method which broadly works on a percentage of taxable income against all receipts including any exempt income.

Many disputes have arisen as to whether VAT on purchases is attributable to taxable (fully recoverable), residual (partially recoverable) or exempt supplies (irrecoverable).

The taxpayer usually contends that VAT relates to taxable supplies rather than being part of the business overheads, or part of business overheads rather than exempt supplies, thereby increasing VAT recovery. Customs on the other hand argue that VAT relates to business overheads rather than taxable supplies, or exempt supplies rather than business overheads, thereby decreasing VAT recovery.

Sheffield Co-operative Society Ltd (1987)

It was held that VAT on refurbishment costs was not recoverable as they related to an exempt licence to occupy land. The partially exempt company operated a department store and spent money on refurbishing a restaurant which it intended to let to an independent operator. The company had argued that the VAT should be recoverable as relating to an intention to improve sales in the adjacent taxable department store.

C & E Commrs v Deutsche Ruck UK Reinsurance Co Ltd (1995)

A partially exempt insurance company recovered in full VAT on legal fees it incurred resisting a claim under a zero-rated policy. A compromise agreement was eventually reached with the claimant. Customs consider the VAT should have been treated as residual as it was a general overhead of the business. The tribunal allowed the appeal holding that the VAT had been used in the making of a taxable supply and was therefore fully deductible.

West Lothian College SPV Ltd (2002)

A college leased land to a company which was to construct a building and sub-lease the land back to the college. The company was also contracted to provide a 25-year maintenance service to the college in respect of the building. The company recovered part of its VAT on the construction contending that it had provided both taxable maintenance services as well as exempt land supplies. The tribunal allowed the appeal.

[The *Southern Primary Housing Ltd* (2004) case casts doubt on whether this treatment would be successful on other similar developments.]

Southampton Leisure Holdings (2002)

A partially exempt company treated VAT on professional fees related to the purchase of the share capital of a professional football club as residual tax and thereby had a partial recovery of the VAT concerned. Customs assessed the company on the basis that the VAT was related to the exempt purchase of shares. The company argued that the VAT related to the intention of the company to make taxable supplies of management services to the football club and therefore the VAT should be apportioned. The appeal was allowed in part to the extent that the VAT related to the general purposes of the business. VAT recovery on some of the professional fees was disallowed on the basis that the advice concerned the exempt purchase of shares.

Cooper & Chapman (Builders) Ltd v C & E Commrs (1993)

A large house was converted and advertised as holiday accommodation. All the VAT on the conversion was recovered. Subsequently, the house was let in part to an American company to house employees. The court held that as part of the supply of the property had changed from the provision of holiday accommodation to the exempt supply of a lease, Customs were right to assess for a proportion of the VAT originally recovered.

1.16.4 Capital Goods Scheme

The Capital Goods Scheme applies to certain capital assets, including land and buildings, that are 'used up' by a business over a number of years. The scheme recognises the fact that there may be variations in the extent to which such assets are used for taxable business purposes over the lifespan of the asset. The VAT recovery position is therefore monitored annually over a ten-year period.

Broadly, the scheme applies where VAT has been paid in relation to the following:

- the purchase or self-supply of land or a building where the value of the supply exceeds £250,000 and where VAT must be accounted for by the seller; or

- the construction, extension or refurbishment of a building where the value of construction works exceeds £250,000.

The scheme operates as follows:

- In the year of acquiring the asset or incurring the construction expenditure, the VAT incurred is recovered on the basis of the use of the asset for taxable activities (i.e. based on the 'partial exemption' recovery calculation).

- If the extent of taxable use changes in each of the first ten years of ownership, then an annual adjustment must be made using a calculation defined in the legislation.

- If the building is sold within the ten-year period, a further adjustment must be made in the year of sale, including the normal annual adjustment outlined above; and additionally, depending on whether the sale is VAT standard-rated or exempt, a further calculation is made which may lead to a further adjustment.

In addition, there are anti-avoidance rules that need to be considered.

Verbond van Nederlandse Ondernemingen v Inspecteur der Invoerrechten en Accijnzen (1976)

Capital goods were described as goods having the following characteristics: use for the purposes of some business activity; identifiable by their durable nature and value; and acquisition costs not normally treated as current expenditure but written off over several years.

Whitbread Harrowden Settlement (Trustees of) (and related appeals) (1999)

Trustees, who administered an estate, reclaimed VAT relating to some land that was sold due to the construction of a by-pass. The tribunal upheld Customs assessment to recover the tax, holding that as the land was a capital asset of the business, no VAT recovery was possible as the VAT legislation was clear that the sale should be ignored for VAT recovery purposes.

Centralan Property Ltd v C & E Commrs (2003)

A university constructed a building which it sold to a subsidiary company and leased it back. As the sale of a new building is VAT standard-rated, the university reclaimed all the input tax which it had incurred on constructing the building. At a later date, the subsidiary granted a 999-year lease to another company and sold the freehold to the University. Customs said the building was a capital item so VAT recovery was restricted.

[The law has since been amended to prevent such arrangements succeeding in the future.]

1.16.5 Non-deductible input tax

Some VAT is still irrecoverable even if it is related to taxable supplies. The VAT legislation specifically blocks VAT recovery on certain purchases including expenditure on business entertainment, cars, road fuel and certain goods in dwellings.

The items in new dwellings upon which VAT cannot be recovered by the developer include:

- free-standing, prefabricated or fitted furniture excluding kitchens and very basic storage facilities which utilise part of the fabric of the building or which have a primary function not related to being a piece of furniture;
- electrical and gas appliances to the extent that they are not used to provide heat, water or ventilation to the property; and
- carpets.

Jones (1994)

It was held that a developer could not recover VAT on the purchase of free-standing furniture, kitchen appliances and fittings in connection with the sale of newly constructed houses.

Rialto Homes plc (1999)

It was accepted that VAT could be reclaimed on the landscaping element of a housing development to the extent that this was adopted by the local authority but not on the landscaping to the actual houses themselves.

1.17 TAX AVOIDANCE

Tax avoidance is not illegal but it is resisted very strongly by Customs and often leads to legal proceedings being brought. Tax avoidance should be distinguished from tax evasion, which relates to the fraudulent and dishonest non-payment of tax. Severe penalties and imprisonment face those convicted of evasion.

Customs have stated that they will act to close avoidance schemes where possible. They have said that they accept tax mitigation, but not tax avoidance. Tax mitigation is considered to be where a business is structured in a VAT-efficient way without offending the underlying intentions of the VAT legislation in question by giving unfair advantage to the businesses concerned.

IR Commrs v Duke of Westminster (1936)

This case included the famous words, '... every man is entitled if he can to order his affairs so that the tax attaching ... is less than it otherwise would be.'

Ramsay v IR Commrs (1981)

This case concerned a capital gains tax avoidance scheme. It was necessary to ascertain the true legal nature of transactions and then look at the wording of the relevant tax legislation. The 'loss' created in this case was not a true loss as it had no real commercial consequences.

There must be a series of preordained transactions with an intermediate step being inserted for no commercial purpose apart from the avoidance of the liability to tax. The tax avoidance step must be ignored and the tax statute applied accordingly.

Furniss v Dawson (1984)

This case developed the application of the principles established in the *Ramsay* (1981) case.

IR Commrs v Challenge Corp Ltd (1986)

The distinction between tax avoidance and tax mitigation was discussed.

MacNiven v Westmoreland Investments Ltd (2001)

It was held that one had to have regard for the tax legislation and determine whether parliament intended the particular words to have the meaning attached to them. It was stated that there was no such thing as Ramsay principle, more an approach.

Halifax plc (2001)

In what is seen as a landmark tribunal, it was found that a series of transactions entered into by Halifax plc to remove an otherwise irrecoverable VAT cost on the construction of call centres was purely concerned with VAT avoidance; as such, the tribunal sought to deny successful operation of the scheme. The case has been referred to the ECJ to determine (1) whether transactions carried out solely to enable VAT recovery constitute an 'economic activity' under the Sixth VAT Directive, and (2) whether the doctrine of 'abuse of rights' applies in VAT to disallow VAT recovery. The opinion of the Advocate General rejected the 'economic activity' argument but did give support to the applicability of the 'abuse of rights' principle. The decision of the UK courts is awaited.

Laurie (t/a The Peacock Montessori Nursery) (2001)

This is the first case in which the principles established in the *Halifax* (2002) case were used to counter a lease and lease back tax planning scheme. The tribunal decided that the case was indistinguishable from *Halifax* and dismissed the taxpayer's appeal accordingly.

RBS Property Developments Ltd; Royal Bank of Scotland Group plc (2002)

This was another case involving a set of arrangements which in part were implemented to mitigate VAT costs. Customs tried to apply the principles established in the *Halifax* case and disallow recovery of VAT on the basis that the sole or predominant purpose of the transactions was to circumvent the 'spirit and purpose' of the VAT legislation. The tribunal allowed the appeal by the taxpayer as they considered the transactions were not solely entered into to avoid tax. Legislation has been introduced to prevent this type of corporate structure giving enhanced VAT recovery for exempt businesses.

Recent developments

Legislation was introduced from 1 August 2004 which requires taxpayers to notify Customs when they use certain listed VAT avoidance schemes or they implement arrangements that have the 'hallmarks' of VAT avoidance. The legislation details which schemes or arrangements have to be notified, when they should be notified and how notification must be made.

Of particular relevance to property transactions are listed schemes 1 and 4:

- *Scheme 1* – claiming VAT on refurbished buildings by attributing the tax incurred to a zero-rated major interest grant in the building to a connected person. This could affect residential landlords, student halls of residence and certain charitable use buildings.

- *Scheme 4* – leaseback agreements which aim to defer or reduce the VAT cost of acquiring goods by a business that cannot recover all of the VAT charged to it on those goods.

The 2005 Budget introduced a further listed scheme regarding structures that seek to utilise the disapplication of the option to tax to gain a tax advantage.

1.18 INSOLVENCY

Where insolvency practitioners become involved with the disposal of property they need to ascertain the correct VAT position to ensure they do not become accountable for incorrect VAT treatment.

Law of Property Act ('LPA') Receivers are appointed by lenders in cases where borrowers default on the loan. The LPA Receiver becomes the agent of the borrower and any VAT is dealt with under the borrower's VAT position.

In some circumstances, lenders can become the agent of the borrower. The VAT costs are charged onto the borrower with the bad debt relief rules utilised to recoup the VAT accounted for to Customs by the lender. This VAT recovery only applies to the costs of disposing of the property for the borrower.

Leeds and Holbeck Building Society (1996)

It was held that the costs of obtaining a possession order and securing a property were recoverable by the lender where the sale of the property concerned was subject to VAT.

Sargent v C & E Commrs (1995)

Although it is usually the borrower who accounts for VAT in a LPA Receivership situation, Customs sometimes require the LPA Receiver to do so if the borrower refuses to comply with his VAT obligations.

Glenshane Construction Services Ltd (in liquidation) (1995)

A construction company went into liquidation. The liquidator received further payments but did not account for VAT on them arguing that the company had never issued VAT invoices so no VAT was due. The tribunal held that VAT was to be accounted for when payment was received.

1.19 COLLECTION AND ADMINISTRATION

It has been announced that VAT and all other taxes are to be administered and managed in the UK by a new government department known as HM Revenue & Customs. This comprises the formerly separate departments of the Inland Revenue and HM Customs and Excise. For the purposes of this text the abbreviation 'Customs' has been used to denote the department charged with the 'care and management' of the VAT regime.

Customs have substantial powers and will impose penalties and interest charges if the rules are not followed correctly by taxpayers. A substantial amount of information on Customs' interpretation of VAT is available on the HM Revenue & Customs website, at www.hmrc.gov.uk in the form of Public Notices, Information Sheets and Business Briefs.

1.19.1 Assessments

Customs can raise an assessment against a taxpayer for a variety of reasons including failure to make returns or keep the necessary records and incorrect or incomplete returns. Customs must raise the assessment to the best of their judgment. There are specific time limits within which assessments can be made with a three-year backstop. In the case of fraud, the time limit is 20 years.

Making an assessment to the best of the commissioners' judgment means that they must fairly consider all material before them and base their decision upon that material. The decision reached must also be reasonable.

If Customs become aware of a VAT issue within two years of a return period, Customs are always 'in time'. After the two years have passed, Customs must raise an assessment within 12 months of receipt of relevant information up to a maximum of three years after the relevant return period.

Van Boeckel v C & E Commrs (1981)

In a Scottish case, it was held acceptable, where tax had been undeclared for a period of five years, to base the assessment on a sample period of three months. It was a matter of fact for the tribunal to decide whether 'best judgment' has been exercised.

House (t/a P & J Autos) v C & E Commrs (1995)

An assessment must precisely define the period of time to which it relates. It has been held that the absence of dates from the assessment itself with reference to dates on accompanying schedules is acceptable.

C & E Commrs v Croyden Hotel & Leisure Co Ltd (1996)

A taxpayer claimed back VAT in a VAT return somewhat later than when the supply was made as there was no invoice at the time. Customs consented that this was acceptable. However, it transpired that the VAT reclaimed related to a compensation payment and therefore there was no right of recovery. Customs raised an assessment to recoup the VAT. The taxpayer claimed the assessment was 'out of time'. It was held the assessment was in time as it runs from the VAT return period when the VAT was actually reclaimed and not from when it should have been received.

Inchcape Management Services Ltd (2000)

A transaction, the VAT liability of which was not clear, was omitted from a VAT return. When it was clear that VAT was due, the company paid the VAT and wrote to Customs with full details of the transaction. Once the three-year limit had expired, the company wrote again asking for confirmation that no assessment could be raised. The tribunal held that Customs already had enough information and that there was no dishonesty so no assessment could be raised at that time.

Pegasus Birds Ltd v C & E Commrs (2000)

An assessment was raised which the company argued was made more than 12 months after Customs had sufficient information upon which to base a ruling. The court rejected the company's claim.

1.19.2 Penalties

There are a variety of penalties which Customs can impose if a taxpayer does not comply with the requirements of the VAT regime.

Criminal fraud

This would have to be the result of criminal proceedings. If a person takes steps to avoid tax or to enable another person to do so, a prison sentence or fine is possible.

Dishonest conduct

This is a civil matter and the penalty is 100% of the tax involved. This may be mitigated if the taxpayers co-operate with Customs.

Stevenson and Telford Building & Design Ltd v C & E Commrs (1995)

Not being registered for VAT does not mean a person cannot be fined for failure to comply with the VAT legislation.

Stuttard (t/a De Wynns Coffee House) (1997)

A coffee shop owner failed to keep records to support the case that one third of his sales were zero-rated. The High Court held that the continued allocation on this basis, and the fact the café owner knew the allocation to be incorrect, amounted to reckless dishonesty.

Georgiou t/a Marios's Chippery v United Kingdom (2001)

This case considered whether civil 'dishonest conduct' penalties are criminal in nature because of their severity, including the fact that proof is required beyond reasonable doubt rather than on the balance of probabilities.

Misdeclaration

Misdeclarations of tax in excess of certain limits or of a repeated nature may be penalised by a civil penalty of 15%

of the error if the taxpayer does not make a voluntary disclosure.

Late registration

There is a penalty of between 5% and 15% of the net tax due for the period of default.

Whitehead (1975)

A business failed to register for VAT at the correct time. It was held that Customs were obliged to backdate the registration.

Default Surcharge

A late VAT return or payment of VAT payment can lead to warnings and penalties if repeated missing of deadlines occurs.

Breach of regulations

There are other penalties for failure to keep or retain relevant records and for issuing incorrect certificates.

Mitigation

The above penalties (excluding default surcharges) can be reduced by mitigation. This means Customs or the tribunal can reduce a penalty. However, insufficiency of funds, the amount of tax loss, or acting in good faith, are not matters that can generally be relied upon to reduce a penalty.

Reasonable excuse

Penalties can often be reduced if the taxpayer can demonstrate 'reasonable excuse' for their actions. Reasonable excuse specifically excludes lack of funds and reliance on third parties for advice.

Neal v C & E Commrs (1988)

A model sought reasonable excuse as defence for her failure to register for VAT. It was held that ignorance of the law was a reasonable excuse in this case.

Electric Tool Repair Ltd (1986)

A director bought an off-the-shelf company which he believed was already registered for VAT. This was accepted as a reasonable excuse for late registration.

Jenkinson (1987)

A businessman who thought his accountant had registered him for VAT rang Customs to ask why he had not yet received a VAT return. Customs had not heard of him and tried to impose a penalty. It was held that the businessman had acted in a business like way and as such had a reasonable excuse.

C & E Commrs v Steptoe (1992)

A contractor, who was paid consistently late by a local authority, claimed 'reasonable excuse' for late payments of VAT to Customs. It was held in this case that insufficiency of funds was a reasonable excuse as the contractor had done all he could to pressurise the authority to pay in a more timely fashion.

1.19.3 VAT rulings

VAT rulings can take the form of published guidance from Customs, agreements with Trade Associations and specifically requested rulings by individual taxpayers. The obtaining of a timely and specific ruling can be challenging, and often it is more practical for parties to a transaction to introduce warranties or indemnities into contractual arrangements.

Elstead (Thursley Road) Recreational Trust (2004)

The Trust received a ruling that a building it was constructing for two village sports clubs was VAT standard-rated. The ruling also stated that the Trust had the right of appeal. The tribunal held that there was no right of appeal as the construction works had not commenced.

F & I Services Ltd v C & E Commrs (2001)

In a case concerning vouchers sold to purchasers of second-hand cars, the company had obtained a ruling from Customs saying that the car dealers did not have to account for VAT on their supply of vouchers. Customs subsequently withdrew this ruling saying it was incorrect and asked that they account for VAT on all future supplies. The company applied for a judicial review in respect of the revised ruling. This application was rejected. The judge held that taxpayers cannot have any legitimate expectation that Customs will administer VAT in any way which is contrary to law. The taxpayer's only legitimate expectation was that it would not be asked to pay tax in respect of past transactions.

1.19.4 Extra-statutory concessions

Public Notice 48 *Extra-statutory concessions* published by Customs contains a list of specific circumstances where Customs recognise that strict application of VAT law creates a disadvantage or an unintended effect. In these cases, those affected may rely on published extra-statutory concessions to the extent they are relevant to their particular circumstances. In the context of VAT rulings, sections 3.4 (VAT: Misunderstanding by a VAT Trader) and 3.5 (VAT: Misdirection of the Notice) are relevant.

The misdirection concession stems from the following parliamentary answer made by Mr Robert Sheldon on 21 July 1978 when he said:

> 'Where it is established that an officer of Customs and Excise, with the full facts before him, has given a clear and

unequivocal ruling on VAT in writing, or it is established that an officer knowing the full facts has misled a trader to his detriment, the Commissioners of Customs and Excise would only raise an assessment based on the correct ruling from the date the error was brought to the attention of the registered person concerned.'

This principle has been confirmed as applying to both telephone and written enquiries to Customs.

R v C & E Commrs ex parte Greenwich Property Ltd (2001)

A university recovered VAT on the basis that it had made zero-rated supplies in connection with the provision of accommodation for students. The university relied upon an extra-statutory concession that enabled it to ignore use of the accommodation in vacations for business purposes. Customs said they would not apply the concession and raised an assessment for VAT. It was held that the university was entitled to rely upon the concession.

1.19.5 Complaints

Where Customs have made mistakes, caused delays, given poor or misleading advice or guidance, or their staff behaviour has been unsatisfactory; there is a regional complaints procedure which aims to put right such matters. Details of these procedures are contained in Customs' Notice 1000 *Complaints and putting things right: our code of practice.*

Other alternatives include referral to the Independent Adjudicator, submitting a complaint to the relevant Minister of Parliament or to the Parliamentary Ombudsman.

Complaints of this nature will not generally be considered concurrently with a matter that has been referred to the VAT and Duties Tribunal.

1.19.6 Disputes

Local reconsideration

The first course of action for a taxpayer in possession of a disputed ruling or assessment may be to ask for a local reconsideration. This request should be made in writing within 30 days of the disputed decision with information to enable Customs to reconsider. The taxpayer should also ask Customs to extend the usual time limit for an appeal.

If Customs give a revised decision which is not agreed by the taxpayer, the taxpayer has 30 days to appeal against this to the VAT tribunal provided Customs have agreed to extend the time limit for an appeal. If, however, Customs confirm their original decision then the taxpayer must lodge any appeal within 21 days from the date of confirmation of the original decision.

VAT and Duties Tribunal

A taxpayer has the right of appeal to the independent VAT and Duties Tribunal against certain decisions or assessments made by Customs. Details of the instances where an appeal is possible are set out in the VAT legislation. In order to be valid an appeal must be made in writing within appropriate time limits. Decisions made by the tribunal are binding on the parties concerned but do not create legal precedent.

Higher courts

Appeals from the VAT and Duties Tribunal can be made to the High Court or Court of Appeal on a point of law. Decisions will create legal precedent.

House of Lords

Where clarification on a point of law is of public importance an appeal may be made to the House of Lords. This is the highest English court.

European courts

The UK courts are able to refer questions to the European Court of Justice (ECJ) to aid interpretation of the Sixth VAT Directive.

1.20 MISCELLANEOUS

1.20.1 Interaction with other taxes

1.20.1.1 Taxes generally

In calculating taxable profits, chargeable gains or the extent of capital allowances, a business may include irrecoverable VAT as part of their costs where the VAT relates to allowable expenses of the business concerned. There may be a need for periodical adjustments where assets are subject to the Capital Goods Scheme.

1.20.1.2 Stamp Duty Land Tax

Stamp Duty Land Tax ('SDLT') is chargeable on the VAT-inclusive value of the property concerned. If a property is capable of being opted to tax then SDLT is due on the price inclusive of any VAT that could be chargeable. If, for example, it is the intention of a landlord granting a lease that the option to tax should not be exercised then there should be a clause to that effect in the sale agreement. This will remove obligation to account for SDLT on the potential VAT component of the purchase price.

Glenrothes Development Corp v Inland Revenue Commrs (1994)

It was held that stamp duty was payable on the consideration paid for some land and this included the VAT element of the consideration as the vendor had opted to tax.

1.20.2 Damages

1.20.2.1 Liquidated damages

Liquidated damages clauses are often contained in construction contracts to provide for a fixed monetary penalty to be levied in the event of breach of contract.

For VAT purposes, these damages do not change the value of the construction services provided. VAT must therefore be accounted for on the full value of the supply. The recipient of the liquidated damages does not have to account for VAT on the amount received.

Holiday Inns (UK) Ltd (1993)

A payment of liquidated damages for the loss of future income did not represent consideration for a taxable supply.

1.20.2.2 Compensation

The payment of compensation is generally accepted as being outside the scope of VAT.

This is applicable to compensation under the terms of the *Landlord and Tenant Act* 1954 or the *Agricultural Tenancies Act* 1995 or where a payment is made as a result of legal proceedings.

In cases where there are no court proceedings, or a settlement is reached in relation to some construction work, or the relinquishing of rights under a tenancy, then the payment will be within the scope of VAT. Whether VAT is due will depend on the characteristics of the supply so made.

Garnham (t/a Pro-Mac Surfacing) (1998)

A road surfacing subcontractor was owed money by a civil engineering company. A dispute ensued and eventually an agreement was reached and a payment made to the subcontractor. The subcontractor did not account for VAT on the payment on the basis that the payment was compensation and outside the scope of VAT. It was held that the payment was for works done and as such VAT would be applicable.

Navydock Ltd (2003)

A company purchased a landfill site close to a city centre which was considered to have development potential and obtained planning permission conditional on the site being decontaminated. A dispute arose with the vendor of the contaminated site about the level of contamination and the cost of the clean up. The vendor eventually paid £2.7m of the decontamination costs. Customs issued an assessment charging VAT on this payment. The company argued successfully that this payment was not consideration for any supply of services by them to the vendor and was therefore not subject to VAT.

Cooper Chasney Ltd (1989)

In settling a dispute, one party made a payment to the other in return for being able to use a particular trading name and brand. It was held that VAT should be accounted for on the payment.

Richards (1986)

It was held that a payment made to an architect for work carried out on an abandoned project was consideration for the works he had completed and VAT was chargeable. The architect had argued that the payment represented compensation.

1.21 LOCAL AUTHORITIES AND OTHER GOVERNMENTAL BODIES

Under sections 33 and 41 of the VAT Act 1994, there are provisions for certain government departments to claim refunds of VAT incurred on their non-business statutory activities. In some instances, there are conditions attached as to which expenditure can qualify for refund. VAT recovery also extends to exempt business activities provided the total value of VAT is insignificant when compared to the total VAT recovery made by the department concerned.

Where these government organisations carry out other non-statutory business activities, they are required to account for VAT in the same way as normal commercial enterprises.

The European basis for these rules stems from Article 4(5) of the Sixth VAT Directive which states that bodies such as local authorities shall not be considered as taxable persons in respect of activities which they engage in as public authorities. The exception is when they provide services which would lead to significant distortions of competition in which case they shall be treated as taxable persons.

Mayor & Burgesses of the London Borough of Haringey v C & E Commrs (and cross-appeal) (1995)

After destruction in a fire, Alexandra Palace was rebuilt by a local authority. The VAT on the rebuilding costs was reclaimed under the provisions of section 33 of the VAT Act 1994. Customs subsequently tried to recover this VAT contending that the expenditure in rebuilding the Palace was attributable to the exempt hire of the Palace as an exhibition centre. It was held that the VAT attributable to the exempt supplies was an insignificant proportion of the total tax and as such could be ignored. Thus the VAT recovery was legitimate.

Glasgow City Council (1998)

It was held that repair works carried out by a local authority to a number of buildings where the owners had failed to comply with statutory repair notices were eligible for a refund of VAT under section 33 of the VAT Act 1994. The works were not in the course of any business, were not related to any taxable supply by the authority and had a compulsory element to them in that the authority was exercising its statutory duties under the *Housing (Scotland) Act* 1987.

Rhondda Cynon Taff County Borough Council (2000)

A local authority reclaimed VAT on costs associated with the provision and maintenance of cemeteries. Customs argued that this was a VAT exempt business activity and thus no VAT recovery was possible under section 33 of the VAT Act 1994. The tribunal agreed with the local authority allowing VAT recovery stating that the Council provided and maintained the cemeteries as a public authority and there would be no distortion of competition as there were no equivalent businesses in the private sector likely to be affected.

West Devon District Council v C & E Commrs (2001)

It was held that when a local authority leased a site to a company formed to operate a community arts centre and then constructed the new arts centre, it was not able to recover VAT under the special VAT rules for local authorities. The court held that the grant of the lease was a business transaction and the transaction was not related to any special regime or statutory duties applicable to local authorities.

Stirling Council (2000)

It was held that VAT was not reclaimable by a local authority on some construction works where it purchased some land and agreed as part of the deal to construct a building for the vendor of the land. It was held that the transaction was a matter of 'private law' and that the Council was not acting under a 'special regime applicable to public authorities' hence the section 33 VAT refund rules did not apply.

Isle of Wight Council (2004)

The High Court has referred this case regarding off-street parking charges by a local authority back to the tribunal to consider distortion of competition issues. The tribunal had ruled that off-street parking was provided by a local authority under a public law regime and therefore VAT was not chargeable. The tribunal also ruled that the relevant

European legislative provisions were not implemented in national law, so Customs were not entitled to raise any arguments concerning distortions of competition. The High Court has allowed Customs to argue the distortion of competition point. Customs consider there is distortion of competition and that VAT should be accounted for on the supply.

1.22 SCOTTISH LAW

Since the introduction of VAT there have been various amendments to the VAT legislation to overcome anomalies arising because of differences between land law in Scotland and that of England, Wales and Northern Ireland.

The Scottish equivalent of the English freehold is the dominium utile.

A contract to dispose of land is the same as missives in Scotland. The missives create a personal right, rather than any equitable interest in the land and therefore, the vendor can still sell to a third party at this time.

The completion of a land transaction in Scotland is by way of a formal document known as a disposition. This transfer of the ownership of the land takes place when the disposition is registered in the Register of Sasines or Land Register of Scotland.

Reference to 'fee simple' in the VAT legislation means, in relation to Scottish land law, the estate or interest of the proprietor of the dominium utile or, in the case of land not held on feudal tenure, the estate or interest of the owner.

A 'major interest' means the estate or interest of the proprietor of the dominium utile or, in the case of land not held on feudal tenure, the estate or interest of the owner, or the lessee's interest under a lease for a period of not less than 20 years.

The Scottish equivalent of a 'restrictive covenant' is a 'servitude' and the release of a restrictive covenant is by way of a 'minute of waiver'.

A Scottish partnership is recognised as a legal entity distinct from its partners so in this respect is easier to deal with for VAT purposes than a partnership under English law.

Margrie Holdings Ltd v C & E Commrs (1991)

Under Scottish law if a person enters into a contract (a missive) to purchase land they do not have an interest in land. Under old VAT legislation, this led to the position where a sub-sale of a property created a VAT charge for the party making the sub-sale because they did not ever have an interest in the land. This case led to an amendment to the law to take account of differences between English and Scottish land law.

2
Commercial property

2.1 INTRODUCTION

The basic rule regarding land and property transactions is that the supply of any interest in or right over land, or any licence to occupy land, is exempt for the purposes of VAT unless:

- the supply is of the freehold of a 'new' or incomplete commercial building or civil engineering works;

- the supply is one of the specific exceptions listed in the legislation (including hotel accommodation, car parking, and so on); or

- the supply is of a commercial building or land that is subject to the 'option to tax';

in which cases, the supplies are VAT standard-rated, at 17.5%; or

- the supply is of the first grant of a 'major interest' in:
  - a residential dwelling or a building used for a 'relevant residential purpose' or a 'relevant charitable purpose' and the supply is made by the person constructing the building; or
  - a non-residential building converted to residential dwelling(s) or to a building used for a 'relevant residential purpose', where the supply is made by the person converting the building; or
  - a 'substantially reconstructed' protected building by the person undertaking the reconstruction works; or
  - an existing residential building that has been derelict for a period in excess of ten years, prior to the granting of the 'major interest';

in which cases, the supplies are zero-rated.

Other supplies may be outside the scope of VAT such as a transfer of a going concern, some inducement payments and rent-free periods.

2.2 VAT-EXEMPT SUPPLIES OF LAND

Article 13B(b) of the Sixth Directive states that the leasing or letting of immoveable property shall be exempt from VAT. Items (g) and (h) of Article 13B also provide that certain supplies of land, buildings and parts of buildings shall be exempt from VAT.

The closest corresponding provision in the UK legislation states that the 'grant of any interest in or right over land or of any licence to occupy land' is exempt from VAT (VAT Act 1994, Schedule 9, Group 1, item 1).

There are many exceptions to the basic position stated above.

EC Commission v United Kingdom (1997)

It was emphasised that the exemption from VAT provided for the leasing and letting of immoveable property is to be interpreted strictly since it constitutes an exception to the general principle that VAT is chargeable on all services supplied for consideration by a taxable person.

Stichting 'Goed Wonen' v Staatssecretaris van Financiën (1999)

'Leasing' was explained to have the characteristics of conferring on the person concerned, for an agreed period and for payment, the right to occupy property as if that person were the owner and to exclude any other person from enjoyment of such a right.

Blasi v Finanzamt München (1995)

The leasing or letting of immoveable property is exempt from VAT. In the hotel sector, however, the provision of accommodation is removed from the exemption and VAT is charged. It was held that the scope of the standard rating cannot be interpreted strictly. This is because the intention of the VAT system generally is that VAT shall be charged wherever possible. On the other hand, the land VAT exemption should be interpreted strictly.

National Provincial Bank Ltd v Ainsworth (1965)

A right over some land must amount to at least a legal or equitable interest in that land. This distinguishes the words 'any interest in or right over land' from a 'licence to occupy land' in the VAT legislation. A licence to occupy would not amount to a legal or equitable interest.

2.2.1 Licence to occupy

A licence to occupy land is exempt from VAT subject to the option to tax.

The words 'licence to occupy' are contrasted from the words 'grant of any interest in or right over land'. Whereas an interest or right will give legal rights of access to that land a licence will not necessarily give rights over the land itself, although there will be a right to sue the licensor if the licensee was denied the benefits of any agreement entered into.

Customs say that in order for a licence to occupy to exist there must be the following characteristics within any agreement – payment by the licensee to the licensor for that licensee to use a specified piece of land even if the exact area can be varied and others may enter the specified land when not being used by the licensee.

Customs also say that a licence to occupy may not be created where there is no exclusive area of use, the land value is negligible in comparison to the facilities available or there is a supply of the right to locate a coin-operated machine whether fixed or not.

Rochdale Hornets Football Club Co Ltd (1975)

The distinction between 'grant of any interest in or right over land' and 'licence to occupy land' was highlighted, and further that a 'licence to occupy land' was different from a licence generally relating to land. Members of the public, who purchased a programme and were permitted to watch a rugby game as standing spectators were not being granted a 'licence to occupy', thus the supply fell outside the VAT exemption and VAT was due on the entry fee.

Trewby v C & E Commrs (1976)

The distinction between licence to occupy land and a licence to use facilities was made. Members of a club who were granted rights to use the club's grounds and facilities were not being granted a licence to occupy the grounds, but a licence to use the facilities. This in turn meant that VAT was due on the charges made.

Lubbock Fine & Co v C & E Commrs (1992)

As part of the conclusions of this case, the Advocate General stated that a 'letting of immoveable property' includes a licence.

Staatssecretaris van Financiën v Coffeeshop Siberië vof (1998)

In commenting on the case, the Advocate General said that he did not consider the renting of a table in an Amsterdam coffee shop amounted to a letting of immoveable property.

C & E Commrs v Sinclair Collis Ltd (2001)

It was held that the grant, by the owner of premises (the site holder) to an owner of a cigarette vending machine, of the right to install, operate and maintain the machine on the premises for a period of two years, in a place nominated by the site holder, in return for a percentage of the gross profits of the sales of cigarettes and other tobacco goods on the premises was not a letting of immoveable property within the meaning of the Sixth VAT Directive. It was stated that the principal element of the agreement was not the occupation of a specific piece of land, but a supply of services of installing a machine.

Wolverhampton and Dudley Breweries plc v C & E Commrs (1990)

This earlier decision considered the VAT liability of the coin-operated amusement machines positioned in pubs. It was held that there was no licence to occupy land. It was considered that the use or enjoyment of the land was not a major consideration to the agreements and that considerations such as maximising beer sales and machine usage were the principal factors in positioning the machines.

Wendy Fair Market Club (1977)

The provision of sites for traders at markets and fairs were held to be licences to occupy and therefore exempt from VAT.

Tameside Metropolitan Borough Council (1979)

The tribunal held that the short duration (ten hours maximum in all) of letting market stalls did not prevent it from qualifying as a licence to occupy land.

Enever (1983)

The provision of a mobile table in a pre-rented hotel room for the purposes of an antiques fair did not amount to the grant of an interest in or right over land or any licence to occupy land, thus the services were chargeable to VAT.

Business Enterprises (UK) Ltd (1988)

The hiring of a furnished room in a business centre which additionally gave the right to use office facilities and amenities amounted to an exempt land supply. The additional facilities were integral to the grant of the licence to occupy and did not constitute a separate taxable supply.

Ultimate Advisory Services Ltd (1993)

It was held that there was no evidence that payments made by a company to an associate company amounted to consideration to rent and exclusively occupy any part of a building owned by the associate company. Therefore, there was no exempt land supply and VAT was chargeable on the supply.

Sovereign Street Workspace Ltd (1992)

In this case, the tribunal held that the supplies made constituted two separate supplies; one of an exempt licence to occupy and one of VAT standard-rated use of facilities such as phone-answering services and mail handling. It was held that these services could be enjoyed irrespective of whether the user occupied space at the premises concerned.

BAA v C & E Commrs (1997)

A right to occupy two shops in an airport terminal was held to be an exempt licence to occupy land.

Abbottsley Golf & Squash Club Ltd (1997)

It was held that exclusivity was not an essential condition in order for there to be a VAT-exempt licence to occupy land. The details of the licence agreement would need to be considered to determine the exact times of exclusivity.

Holmwood House School Developments (2003)

A property developer built a new school building and entered into an agreement with two partnerships to allow use of the new building. The developer argued that there was a VATable supply of facilities. Customs argued there was a VAT-exempt licence to occupy. It was held that there were rights of occupation granted and the supply was exempt from VAT. The effect was that the developer was unable to recover VAT on its development costs.

British Telecommunications plc (1999)

BT installed and maintained payphones on the premises of others. BT argued that the agreement with the site owner amounted to a licence to use the land (VAT standard-rated) as opposed to Customs' suggestion that there was a licence to occupy land (VAT-exempt). The tribunal held that there was a licence to occupy land.

[This decision is now overturned by the *Sinclair Collis* decision.]

Blendhome Ltd (t/a Stanhill Court Hotel) (1999)

It was held that an exclusivity fee payable by wedding parties to secure exclusive use of the public rooms and grounds of a hotel was an enhancement of the supply of the wedding reception facilities and as such would follow the VAT liability of that principal supply. VAT was therefore due on the payment.

2.3   VAT STANDARD-RATED SUPPLIES OF LAND

The UK legislation lists specific exceptions to the land exemption which will be VAT standard-rated (VAT Act 1994, Schedule 9, Group 1, item 1).

In addition to the categories listed below, Article 13B(b) of the Sixth VAT Directive, from which the UK legislation is derived, also includes the letting of permanently installed equipment and machinery and the hire of safes as being VAT standard-rated. For all these exceptions this means that VAT incurred on associated construction and development costs will be recoverable.

The election to waive exemption or 'option to tax' is an additional mechanism by which a person can elect to transform a VAT-exempt land supply into a taxable land supply. This means VAT is chargeable on all future supplies of that property and any VAT incurred in connection with that property is recoverable.

2.3.1 Sale of new commercial buildings

The supply of the freehold of a 'new' or uncompleted commercial building or civil engineering works is VAT standard-rated at 17.5%. An apportionment may be required where VAT-exempt land is also sold.

A building or civil engineering work is 'new' if it was completed less than three years before the sale of the freehold.

A building or civil engineering work is taken as completed when an architect issues a certificate of practical completion, or when the building is fully occupied (whichever comes first).

Wynn Realisations Ltd v Vogue Holdings Inc (1999)

Wynn sold a property to Vogue where the contract held that the price was exclusive of VAT. It was assumed that the sale was exempt from VAT. It was discovered later that the building was 'new' and therefore VAT was due at 17.5%. Wynn paid the VAT to Customs and sought to recover it from Vogue. The court found for Wynn saying that the words 'exclusive of VAT' meant that if VAT was payable then it could be added to the sale price.

Trade Only Plant Sales Ltd (2004)

A company purchased a new commercial property. Two years later the company transferred its business to an associated company as a going concern. The property was retained by the original company which then ceased to be VAT registered. Customs considered that VAT was due on the deemed supply of the property at deregistration as it was 'new' (i.e. less than three years old). Under rules concerning transfers of going concerns the associated company had to pay the VAT.

2.3.1.1 Definition of civil engineering

GKN Birwelco Ltd (1983)

It was held that civil engineering work must require the skills of a civil engineer in order to facilitate its successful completion; it must be work that would be described as civil engineering by the civil engineering profession; the works must be considered as a whole and must not be predominantly the installation of items of plant or machinery. The works might include earth removal or the construction of structures such as bridges, roads, canals, railways, harbours, drainage and swimming pools.

St Aubyn's School (Woodford Green) Trust Ltd (1982)

The construction of a playing field where a substantial amount of the work was excavation, infilling, grading and levelling was held to be civil engineering.

Roskill (1981)

The erection of railings in front of a house was held not to be works of civil engineering.

UFD Ltd (1981)

The clearance of a burial ground did not amount to civil engineering works.

Rawlins Davy & Wells (1977)

The construction of a pavement crossing was held not to be works of civil engineering.

2.3.2 Right to take game or fish

The grant of any interest, right or licence to take game or fish is a taxable supply subject to VAT. If the supply is part of a freehold sale then the liability will follow that of the land. By agreement with Country Landowner's Association in 1991, if the value of gaming or fishing rights exceeds 10% of the value of a leasehold then that right should be valued separately and will be chargeable to VAT.

Carter (2001)

The sale of live pheasants that were bought by customers before the shooting season had begun and left on the seller's land to roam and be fed prior to being shot by the purchasers some months later was held not to be a VAT standard-rated supply of any right to take game. It was held that the supply was zero-rated as a supply of live animals for human consumption.

C & E Commrs v Lord Fisher (1981)

Lord Fisher ran shooting parties for his friends as a hobby. Customs contended that he was in business and should account for VAT on the payments he received to fund the shoots. However, he was held not to have been in business, based on consideration of a number of factors, including the level of commerciality, the continuity of operations, the creation of an entity distinct from its separate parts, the element of organisation, the question of whether the shoots were a 'serious undertaking earnestly pursued', were carried on for some form of payment; and were not being carried out for pleasure or as a hobby.

Chalk Springs Fisheries (1986)

It was held that a trout fishery was making standard-rated supplies of the right to catch fish. The fishery had argued that they were making two supplies –
a standard-rated supply of the right to fish and a zero-rated supply of the trout as food.

C & E Commrs v Parkinson (1989)

It was held that the freehold sale of land or disposition with fishing rights was exempt from VAT. The law relating to the exceptions to the exemption could not be interpreted as including the supply of a freehold for sporting rights; only transfers of lesser interests could be caught by the VAT standard rate. This case, which is applicable to many of the VAT standard-rated exceptions to the VAT exemption, highlights the mismatch between the European legislation and the UK interpretation of those provisions.

2.3.3 Hotels and similar accommodation

The provision of accommodation in hotels, inns, boarding houses or similar establishments is VAT standard-rated. 'Similar establishments' cover premises where there is furnished sleeping accommodation that is deemed to be suitable for use by visitors or travellers. Additionally, accommodation in rooms which are provided in conjunction with sleeping accommodation or for the purpose of a supply of catering are also VAT standard-rated.

The lease of a hotel to a hotel operator will be VAT-exempt subject to the option to tax.

Operators of accommodation where individual guests stay for more than four weeks can zero-rate their supplies for any stay over the four-week limit. This zero-rating can only apply to a maximum of 80% of the charge. Any food or meals supplied are VAT standard-rated.

Namecourt Ltd (1984)

It was held that a company that provided 'bed and breakfast' accommodation for homeless and unemployed people was required to account for VAT on the amounts charged on the basis that the accommodation was 'a hotel, inn, boarding house or similar establishment'.

McGrath v C & E Commrs (1992)

It was held that the proprietor of a boarding house who failed to account for VAT on payments received from long-term residents was liable to account for VAT on the payments received.

Soka Gakkai International UK (1995)

A registered charity which operated a religious centre charged VAT on its supplies of accommodation and reclaimed VAT on expenditure related to the property. It was held that the supplies of accommodation were exempt as the grant of an interest, right or licence to occupy land and therefore the VAT reclaim was not allowable.

International Students House (1996)

International Student House is a charity with the aim of improving international relations by providing facilities for students from varying cultural backgrounds. The charity provided accommodation, counselling and welfare services. A dispute arose after Customs contended that it was providing 'hotel or similar accommodation' and should charge VAT at the standard rate of VAT. The tribunal held that the predominant purpose of the charity was to improve international relations and not the provision of accommodation and therefore no VAT had to be accounted for.

Dinaro Ltd (t/a Fairway Lodge) (1999)

It was held that a lodge used to provide supervised living accommodation principally for people rehabilitating into the outside world after periods in psychiatric institutions was VAT-exempt. Customs had argued that VAT was due on the supplies of accommodation on the basis that the lodge was a 'similar establishment' to a boarding house.

Acorn Management Services Ltd (2001)

It was held that self-catering accommodation provided for overseas university students attending courses in the UK was a 'similar establishment' to a hotel, inn or boarding house and VAT was chargeable. The fact that the accommodation was not openly competing with the hotel sector, was not available to passing trade and was not serviced accommodation did not make it exempt from VAT.

Leez Priory (2003)

A country house and its grounds were made available for wedding functions. The operators wished to retain a Customs ruling that allowed for two separate supplies – a VAT-exempt licence to occupy land and a VAT standard-rated supply of facilities such as catering. It was held that the land supply could not be disassociated from the wedding facilities and there was, therefore, a composite supply of wedding functions which were VAT standard-rated under the definition of 'similar establishment' in the VAT legislation.

BJ Group (2002)

It was held that a large building let on a room-by-room basis to a variety of individuals and companies was a 'similar establishment' to a hotel and VAT was due on the income received by the owners of the building.

North East Direct Access Ltd (2003)

It was held that a hostel for homeless people was not exempt from accounting for VAT as it was offering sleeping accommodation in a similar establishment to an hotel, inn or boarding house. The case was distinguished from *Dinaro Ltd (t/a Fairway Lodge)* (1999) where Dinaro Ltd predominantly accepted persons coming from psychiatric institutions and provided close supervision and care.

2.3.4 **Holiday accommodation**

The grant of any interest in, right over, or licence to occupy holiday accommodation is VAT standard-rated. This category includes any building, hut, caravan, houseboat or tent that is advertised as or held out to be holiday accommodation. It also includes the freehold purchase or leasehold purchase by way of a premium of any 'new' accommodation that cannot be occupied throughout the year or occupied as a principal private residence. 'New' is taken to mean less than three years old. Buildings over three years old will be VAT-exempt.

Haven Leisure Ltd (1990)

This case led to a change in the law such that the sale of the freehold or long leaseholds of new holiday accommodation was to be treated as VAT standard-rated. Previously such sales were held to be VAT-exempt.

Poole Borough Council (1991)

The letting of beach huts and hut sites was held to be VAT standard-rated.

Ashworth (1994)

It was held that ground rates and services charges in association with a lodge occupied for 11 months of the year by a person as their home were exempt from VAT. The lease prevented occupation in the month of February. Customs argued that the supplies should be VAT standard-rated due to the occupancy restriction. The tribunal stated that the accommodation was not chargeable to VAT as it could not be classed as being accommodation in the hotel sector or similar sectors. The tribunal thought the requirements of the UK legislation went beyond those set down in the European legislation.

Livingstone Homes UK Ltd (2000)

It was held in this Scottish case that the sale of holiday dwelling houses were VAT zero-rated as the tribunal considered that the planning conditions did not rule out that use of these holiday properties as a person's principal private residence.

[This decision was considered to be incorrect by the chairman of the subsequent *Loch Tay* tribunal decision.]

Loch Tay Highland Lodges Ltd (2005)

A number of lodges were constructed and then sold. The sale was treated as VAT zero-rated. It was held that due to the restrictions on use in the planning permission zero-rating was not applicable. The planning restricted use to that of holiday accommodation and debarred use as a main or sole residence.

[This contrasts with the decision in *Livingstone Homes UK Ltd* (2000).]

2.3.5 **Seasonal pitches for caravans, tents or camping facilities**

The provision of seasonal pitches for caravans and the provision of facilities to persons to whom pitches are provided at caravan parks are VAT standard-rated.

A seasonal pitch is either a pitch provided for less than one year, or if provided for more than one year, the person to whom it is provided is not allowed to live in a caravan at all times. The restriction may be by way of the terms of any consent, statutory planning consent or other permission.

The provision of pitches for tents or camping facilities is VAT standard-rated.

AE House & Son (1985)

It was held that the winter storage of caravans was a taxable supply as opposed to an exempt supply of a licence to occupy land. There was no occupation of any specified area of land but rather a storage service which was outside the scope of the exemption.

Smith (1994)

It was held that the licence fees charged to caravan holders on a site open from March to October each year were chargeable to VAT and excluded from exemption.

Colaingrove Ltd v C & E Commrs (2004)

This case concerned whether treatment of seasonal caravan pitches as VAT standard-rated by the UK Government was within the limits of the relevant European legislation. It was held that the test of seasonality outlined in the UK legislation was a reasonable one for identifying holiday related caravan sites.

2.3.6 Provision of parking facilities

The grant of facilities for parking a vehicle is VAT standard-rated. This includes the lettings and leasing of parking facilities such as car parks, garages and storage for caravans and bicycles. The freehold sale of such facilities will only be VAT standard-rated if the facilities are less than three years old (i.e. they are 'new'). If it is greater than three years old then the freehold sale would be VAT-exempt with the option to tax.

If parking facilities are provided in association with other premises such as zero-rated residential or VAT-exempt commercial accommodation, then the liability of the parking will follow the liability of the main development if the facilities are provided by the same person.

Fonden Marselisborg Lystbådehavn v Skatteministeriet (2002)

The court held that both water-based mooring berths and storage sites on dry land were 'immoveable property' within Article 13B(b) of the Sixth VAT Directive. They also held that the letting of premises and sites for parking vehicles included boats. Consequently the exemption did not apply and VAT was to be accounted for on the supplies.

Skatteministeriet v Henriksen (1988)

It was held that the letting of parking places, which were closely linked to VAT-exempt lettings of immoveable property, could not be excluded from the VAT exemption.

C & E Commrs v Trinity Factoring Services Ltd (1994)

It was held that a VAT standard-rated grant of facilities for parking a vehicle even though the parties concerned agreed that the purpose of letting the lock up garages was for domestic storage.

Wilson (1977)

It was held that an individual who leased three garages for storage purposes had not been granted VAT-exempt land rights. The garages were within the definition of parking facilities, so that the leases were excluded from exemption and thus VAT standard-rated.

Henley Picture House Ltd (1979)

It was held that a licence granted to a supermarket by a cinema to use land owned by the cinema for parking was subject to VAT as a grant of facilities for parking vehicles.

Inter City Motor Auctions Ltd (1986)

It was held that VAT was due on a charge made by motor vehicle auctioneers to customers for parking up their vehicles that they wished to sell.

Routledge (2004)

Land rented to a football club which provided a means of access to a football ground for spectators and service vehicles was held not to be used as parking facilities and therefore, the rent could be treated as exempt from VAT.

2.3.7 Right to fell or remove timber

The grant of any right to fell and remove standing timber is VAT standard-rated.

2.3.8 Storage of aircraft and boats

The grant of any facilities for housing, or storage of, an aircraft or for the mooring, or storage of, a ship, boat or other vessel is VAT standard-rated. Mooring includes anchoring or berthing.

2.3.9 Seats at sports grounds, theatre, concert halls, etc.

The grant of any right to occupy a box, seat or other accommodation at a sports ground, theatre, concert hall or other place of entertainment is VAT standard-rated.

Southend United Football Club (1997)

A football club issued seasonal licences of executive boxes at its stadium. Rather than treating the entire supply as VAT standard-rated they apportioned the supply between the time the box was used for watching football games and the total time the box was available for use. The non-football viewing time was considered to be attributable to a VAT-exempt licence to occupy land. Customs disagreed. It was held that Customs were correct to raise an assessment as the football club had ignored the value attached to watching the games over the general ability to use the box at other times.

2.3.10   Grant of facilities for playing sport

The grant of facilities for playing any sport or participating in any physical recreation is VAT standard-rated.

The VAT exemption will apply, however, where the grant of the facilities is for:

- a continuous period of use exceeding 24 hours; or

- a series of 10 or more periods, whether or not exceeding 24 hours in total, where the following conditions are satisfied:

  - each period is in respect of the same activity carried on at the same place;

  - the interval between each period is not less than one day and not more than 14 days;

  - consideration is payable by reference to the whole series and is evidenced by written agreement;

  - the grantee has exclusive use of the facilities; and

  - the grantee is a school, a club, an association or an organisation representing affiliated clubs or constituent associations.

There is also an exemption for the grant of facilities to participate in sports supplied by a non-profit-making organisation to an individual.

Colchester School of Gymnastics (1997)

A gymnasium operated by a charity was used by local gymnastic clubs and other organisations. Although initially charging VAT on its letting income, it sought to have these supplies treated as VAT-exempt. It was held that the supplies could not be exempt as exclusive use of the facilities was not available to any party and also that the letting was not to individuals.

Pritchard (t/a Dace at 8) (2002)

A couple operated a dancing school and hired a room for their classes. It was held that they were renting facilities in order to allow participation in a physical recreation and the charge was VAT standard-rated. The couple had argued that the classes were operated as a school and should be VAT-exempt.

2.3.11 Options

The grant of any right including an equitable right; a right under an option or a right of pre-emption; or, in relation to Scotland, a personal right; to call for or be granted an interest or right which would fall within any of the VAT standard-rated supplies above will also be chargeable to VAT at the standard rate of VAT.

2.4 THE OPTION TO TAX

2.4.1 Principles

The basic rule is that the supply of land and buildings subject to certain exceptions is exempt from VAT. However, a taxpayer can elect to waive exemption, or 'opt to tax' as it is more commonly known. This election transforms the VAT-exempt supply of land into a VAT standard-rated supply. VAT must be accounted for on all future receipts from the property, including its eventual sale.

The benefit of making the 'option to tax' is that VAT can then be recovered on expenditure such as refurbishment costs, whereas under an exempt supply this would be irrecoverable.

The tenant will suffer no disadvantage if he or she is operating a fully taxable business, as all VAT paid out will be recoverable. A partially exempt or exempt business will, however, suffer increased costs as it will have to pay irrecoverable VAT to its landlord. This may lead to a discount in the price of the building if potential buyers are likely to be mainly exempt traders such as financial institutions.

The option to tax is irrevocable, as long as the building remains in the same ownership, with the exception that revocation is possible within the first three months (if there is no tax effect) or after 20 years. If the building changes hands, the new owner is not bound or covered by the vendor's option.

Coach House Property Management Ltd (1992)

The tribunal held that member states were entitled, under Article 13B of the Sixth VAT Directive, to set the scope and details of the operation of the option to tax. This includes the provision in UK law that the option is irrevocable.

The option to tax is made on a building-by-building basis and cannot be made for part of a building. A building includes linked buildings. A complex consisting of a number of units grouped around a fully enclosed concourse, such as a shopping mall, is also classed as a single building for the purposes of the 'option to tax' rules.

[At present Customs' policy is that an option to tax disappears when a building is demolished despite the result of the *Breitsohl* case detailed below.]

Finanzamt Goslar v Breitsohl (1998)

The ECJ held that buildings and the land upon which they stand cannot be treated separately for the purposes of the option to tax. In this German case, a car dealer wanted to opt to tax a building but not the land such that she could recover VAT on some building works but not charge VAT on the sale of the underlying land.

Finanzamt Uelzen v Armbrecht (1992)

An opted building comprising commercial and residential accommodation was sold. The German tax authorities said VAT was due on the full proceeds received. The ECJ held that parts of a property not in business use (e.g. the private residential accommodation) would not be subject to the option to tax. VAT would only be accounted for on the commercial parts.

The option to tax can be disapplied in certain circumstances; either where the property comes out of commercial use, or where arrangements contravene any of the anti-avoidance rules designed to prevent undesired VAT avoidance.

2.4.2 Making the option to tax

'Opting to tax', or 'electing to waive exemption', is a two- (and sometimes three-) stage process. First, the decision must be made to opt to tax; then, Customs must be notified of the decision. For the option to be valid, notification must be made within 30 days of the decision. Details of the building and site to be opted should be provided to Customs.

Chalegrove Properties Ltd (2001)

The tribunal held that the option to tax was notified when it was put in the post to Customs rather than on the day it was received by Customs.

In certain circumstances, permission to opt to tax may also be required from Customs, where there are issues regarding the level of VAT recovery that the option will generate. This permission may be given automatically in some cases. The granting of an exempt interest before making an election will mean that some input tax incurred before the election may be irrecoverable.

Blythe Limited Partnership (1999)

This tribunal was concerned with the accidental notification to Customs of the option to tax on 16 properties rather than the four intended. It was held, distinguishing the making of the option from the notification of the option, that the taxpayer was only bound by the making of the option and not the notification stage. Therefore, only four properties were validly opted, as always intended.

Hammersmith & West London College (2002)

The assistant principal of the above college opted to tax three properties owned by the college. Later, the college sold one of the properties without accounting for VAT. The college appealed, contending that the assistant principal did not have the authority to make the option. The tribunal dismissed the college's appeal.

Norbury Developments v C & E Commrs (1999)

Some land upon which the option to tax had been made was purchased and immediately sold with the benefit of planning permission. The intermediary company did not opt to tax the land and Customs denied VAT recovery in connection with the original purchase. The company claimed under European legislation that the sale of building land should be compulsorily VAT standard-rated. It was held that the UK was allowed to retain the VAT exemption under the transitional rules in place.

C & E Commrs v R & R Pension Fund Trustees (1996)

The court held that where a property is let on an exempt basis and then the option to tax is made and that the property falls within the capital goods provisions then the adjustment process uses the Capital Goods Scheme mechanism to recover the VAT over the next ten years rather than the 'fair and reasonable' formula set out in paragraph 3 of Schedule 10 to the VAT Act 1994.

Royal and Sun Alliance Group Insurance Group plc v C & E Commrs (2003)

An insurance company used a building in a VAT-exempt business, the landlord having opted to tax the rent. The VAT on the rent was recovered on a residual basis and continued to be so after the company vacated the building and let it stand empty.

Subsequently, the company opted to tax the building and let it. The company sought to have the VAT incurred in the void period reallocated to the future taxable letting. The House of Lords held this was incorrect and the residual (and less beneficial as far as the company was concerned) basis of recovery was correct.

Classic Furniture (Newport) Ltd (2000)

A subsidiary company acquired a property, paying VAT on the purchase price. The property was immediately transferred to its owner. The owner opted to tax the property and recovered the VAT charged to it by the subsidiary company. Customs said the VAT was not recoverable by the owner as the subsidiary company had not opted to tax the property itself. The subsidiary company requested that a belated notification be accepted. The tribunal accepted that the election had been made and held that the belated notification should be accepted.

C & E Commrs v University of Wales College of Cardiff (1995)

A building owner refurbished a building which it then used for its own VAT-exempt purposes. Later it decided to let the building and an option to tax was made. The builder owner sought to recover some of the VAT on the refurbishment because of the change of use of the property from exempt to taxable purposes. It was held that the method of calculating the attribution of VAT was prescribed by the rules relating to exempt users rather than exempt lettings of the property, thereby producing a less favourable result for the owners.

2.4.3 Disapplication of the option to tax

There are certain circumstances in which the option to tax will not have effect. This can lead to additional costs.

Dwellings

The option to tax will not have effect in relation to a grant if the grant is made in relation to a building or part of a building intended for use as a dwelling or a number of dwellings or solely for a relevant residential or relevant charitable purpose (other than use as an office). A grant relating to a pitch for a residential caravan or facilities for mooring a residential houseboat will also lead to the disapplication of the option to tax. A houseboat is not residential if there is any legal restriction which prevents year-round residence.

White (1998)

A person bought a pub and tried to reclaim VAT on the purchase price paid. The vendor had previously opted to tax the property as they had rented the building to a tenant. Customs sought to restrict VAT recovery by the purchaser on the basis that part of the sale price related to 'a dwelling' and as such the option to tax was disapplied with respect to this part of the building. It was held that there was no dwelling for VAT purposes as the residential accommodation was not self-contained.

Watters (1995)

The purchaser of a disused public house appealed to the VAT tribunal regarding the additional VAT on the sale price. The purchaser contended that the public house was intended for use as a dwelling and the sale should be exempt from VAT. Customs argued that the buyer's intention had not been sufficiently communicated to the vendor and thus VAT was chargeable. The tribunal held that the intention had been communicated and the sale could be treated as VAT-exempt.

Lounds (t/a Lounds Associates) (1996)

A property investor owned a building, which, in part he rented, and in part he occupied for his own business purposes. The building comprised retail units, offices and an empty residential apartment. The owner converted the residential apartment to an office in the hope of finding a tenant and, having opted to tax, recovered the associated VAT. Later the office was converted back to residential use.

In making the election, the owner did not account for VAT on the existing commercial units. The tribunal held that the election had effect over the whole building and VAT was due on all receipts relating to the property. Furthermore, the option could not be disapplied as, at the time of the election, the intention was to use the space for commercial purposes. The subsequent change of intention did not disapply the option.

SEH Holdings Ltd (2000)

A company acquired a disused public house and immediately sold the property on the same day. The original sale was subject to an option to tax and the purchasing company contended the option should not apply because the building was intended for use as a dwelling albeit by the final recipient rather than themselves. The tribunal held in agreeing with Customs that the sale was taxable.

As an exception, where a purchaser of some land intends to use that land for making zero-rated sales of new dwellings, the vendor and purchaser can agree that the option to tax will not be disapplied and the sale will remain VAT standard-rated. The agreement must be in writing and made before the grant takes place.

Housing Associations

The option to tax will not be effective where the grant is to a registered housing association, and that housing association has given the grantor a certificate stating that the land is intended for use as a dwelling, a number of dwellings or solely for relevant residential purposes.

Self-builders

If land is sold to an individual who intends to construct a dwelling for their own occupation otherwise than in the course of a business, the option to tax will be disapplied.

Anti-avoidance restriction

Due to the implementation of various schemes using the option to tax mechanism and lease and leaseback arrangements to help exempt business such as banks and universities remove or mitigate VAT costs on property expenditure anti-avoidance legislation has been introduced.

Test for disapplication of the option to tax

Is the land or building concerned a capital item (or will it become a capital item) for the purposes of the Capital Goods Scheme (i.e. a non-residential building, extension or fitting out contract with costs in excess of £250,000)?

Does the grantor or financier intend or expect use by:

the grantor or financier or a connected person, as defined by section 839 of the *Income and Corporation Taxes Act (ICTA)* 1988;

within the ten-year adjustment period; and

for a non-taxable use (broadly less than 80% taxable)?

If the answer to both of these questions is 'yes', then the option is likely to be disapplied.

Brambletye School Trust Ltd (2002)

A school providing VAT-exempt education services constructed a sports hall and having opted to tax the property leased it to an associate company with a view to recovering the VAT on the construction works. The associate company was to charge VAT to pupils, staff, and the general public for the use of the facilities. It was held that the pupils of the school occupied the building for exempt purposes as part of their education and as such the option to tax was disapplied.

Holmwood House School Developments (2003)

A property developer built a new school building and entered into an agreement with two partnerships to allow use of the new building. The developer argued that there was a VATable supply of facilities. Customs argued there was a VAT-exempt licence to occupy. It was held that there were rights of occupation granted and the supply was exempt from VAT. The effect was that the developer was unable to recover VAT on its development costs. The option to tax was not available as the parties were connected.

East Kent Medical Services Ltd (1998)

A VAT avoidance scheme was implemented which entailed the pre-letting of land prior to the construction of the building, therefore attempting to sidestep the then anti-avoidance rules on the option to tax and VAT recovery. The tribunal held that the scheme was ineffective and the option to tax was disapplied. The law was changed after this case to prevent further arguments regarding interpretation occurring in the future.

Winterthur Life UK Ltd (1998)

The tribunal considered whether pension scheme payments could be seen as 'providing finance' and could lead to the disapplication of the option to tax where payments to a pension fund funded the acquisition of a property. The property acquired in this case was leased to the VAT-exempt business that had made the pension scheme contributions. It was held that although this was an innocent transaction, the anti-avoidance rules must apply. Thus the option to tax was disapplied, preventing the recovery of the VAT incurred.

Fforestfach Medical Centre (2000)

This case concerned the distinction between making an election to waive exemption and notifying the same to Customs. The centre that had not notified Customs of an election requested that a retrospective election be allowed. Whilst a belated notification of an election is allowed this is only the case where no permission is required from Customs. As the centre had made exempt supplies it required Customs permission. Therefore, it was held that no effective election had been made or notified.

Newnham College (2004)

A university college built and renovated their library and leased the library to a subsidiary company which was to provide library services to the college. The college opted to tax the property in order to recover VAT on the construction costs. The tribunal held that Customs were right to disapply the option to tax under the anti-avoidance rules.

2.5 LEASE TRANSACTIONS

There are a number of VAT issues associated with leases. The following table summarises the main supplies associated with leases and the associated VAT treatments.

Lease transactions – table of liabilities

Nature of supply	VAT treatment
LEASE FOR A PREMIUM – tenant pays landlord for a lease.	Exempt supply by the landlord; VAT standard-rated if option to tax exercised by person making the supply.
REVERSE PREMIUM – landlord pays prospective tenant to accept a lease.	If an inducement to accept a lease and associated obligations with no benefit supplied by tenant to landlord then outside scope of VAT; if a benefit passes then it is a VAT standard-rated supply by the landlord.
RENT-FREE PERIOD – landlord offers prospective tenant a rent-free period to accept a lease.	If an inducement to accept a lease and associated obligations with no benefit supplied by tenant to landlord then outside scope of VAT; if a benefit passes then it is a VAT standard-rated supply by the landlord.
SURRENDER – landlord pays tenant to surrender existing lease.	Exempt supply by the tenant; VAT standard-rated if option to tax exercised by person making the supply.
REVERSE SURRENDER – tenant pays landlord to take back the lease.	Exempt supply by the landlord; VAT standard-rated if option to tax exercised by person making the supply.
ASSIGNMENT – third party pays tenant to assign existing lease.	Exempt supply by the tenant (the assignor); VAT standard-rated if option to tax exercised by person making the supply.
REVERSE ASSIGNMENT – Tenant pays third party to take away lease.	Standard-rated supply by the third party (the assignee).

Lease for a premium

Where a lease is granted for a premium, this will be a VAT-exempt supply, unless the landlord has opted to tax, in which case there will be a taxable supply at the standard 17.5% rate of VAT.

Inducements

Payments by landlords to tenants on entering leases have caused many problems when trying to establish the VAT liability. In the past many such payments have been considered to be taxable supplies by the tenant for taking the lease. The 2001 ECJ judgment in the case of *Mirror Group plc* (1998) has clarified this position.

Reverse premiums

A reverse premium is where the landlord pays a prospective tenant to accept a lease. Paragraph 26 of the ECJ *Mirror Group* judgment (1998) held (and it has been accepted by Customs) that where a tenant undertakes for a reverse premium only to become a tenant, pay rent and abide by normal lease obligations, then no VAT supply results.

If, however, the tenant is required to undertake obligations that give rise to benefits to the landlord in addition to the receipt of rent, then Customs consider that a taxable supply of services results. If, for instance, the payment is in any way linked to the performance of a service, such as fitting-out works, then the works will be VAT standard-rated at 17.5%.

C & E Commrs v Mirror Group plc (1998)

Mirror Group plc took a lease of part of a new development and in doing so received a substantial inducement from the landlord. Customs argued that Mirror Group should account for VAT on this payment. Mirror Group disagreed. In its judgment, the ECJ explained that the payment of money to enter a lease alone was outside the scope of VAT, whereas a payment to do something was taxable. It was suggested that the payment could amount to consideration for advertising services, as Mirror Group was effectively an anchor tenant and could attract other tenants into the development. Alternatively, the payment may not relate to any separate and specific obligation by the recipient other than part of the original lease transaction, in which case there is no consideration for any taxable supply.

Gleneagles Hotel plc (1986)

The landlord of a hotel granted a lease to a company, and paid a 'reverse premium' to help the company repair the property. Customs issued an assessment on the basis that the payment was liable to VAT. The company appealed contending that there had been no supply. The tribunal dismissed the company's appeal holding that the payment was consideration paid by the landlord for the company's agreement to provide more valuable benefits under the lease, such as repair and refitting of the hotel.

Neville Russell (1987)

A tenant appealed against an assessment in respect of a payment made to them by the landlord in connection with the renewal of a lease. The payment comprised three components. There was a rent rebate which was accepted as being part of the lease and not a separate supply for VAT purposes (akin to a rent-free period); there was a payment to enable the firm to refurbish the property which was held to be related to a taxable supply of building services [this is supported by the *Mirror Group* decision]; and finally a payment as an inducement to enter into the lease which was held to be a taxable supply [this payment would now be considered to be outside the scope of VAT following the *Mirror Group* decision].

Rent-free periods

Rent-free periods occur when tenants are offered a period of occupancy in which they do not have to pay rent. Where the rent-free period does not relate to any obligations by the tenant for the benefit of the landlord such as carrying out building works then there is no consideration for any supplies by the tenant.

Port Erin Hotels Ltd (1989)

The tribunal held that a rent-free period was given in consideration of the tenant paying for alterations and improvements to hotels. The market value of the works was used to determine the value of the tenant's supply for VAT purposes.

Ridgeons Bulk Ltd v C & E Commrs (1994)

This case considered whether a rent-free period given in consideration of repair and maintenance works was VATable. It was held that it was, as the works completed by the tenant were in consideration for the rental of the building in question, and that VAT must be accounted for by the tenant to Customs.

Surrenders, reverse surrenders and variations to leases

A surrender, where a landlord pays a tenant to surrender a lease before its expiry, is exempt from VAT subject to the possibility of the option to tax by the tenant.

Lubbock Fine & Co v C & E Commrs (1992)

It was held by the ECJ that a payment by a landlord for the surrender of a lease from its tenant was a VAT-exempt payment. Previously, these payments had been treated as taxable under UK VAT law.

A reverse surrender, where a tenant pays a landlord to accept a surrender of a lease before its expiry, is exempt from VAT subject to the possibility of the option to tax by the landlord.

Marbourne Ltd (1994)

A company which occupied an opted building wished to terminate its lease before its expiry and paid the landlord a 'reverse surrender'. It treated this payment as exempt from VAT. In this case the tribunal held that despite the fact the landlord had opted to tax the property the supply could be exempt as the land supply was from the tenant to the landlord.

[This decision was not followed in the subsequent *Central Capital Corporation* tribunal.]

Central Capital Corporation (1994)

It was held that a 'reverse surrender' was a supply of land made by the landlord when he agreed to accept the surrender of the tenant's lease in return for payment. The payment made by the tenant was exempt from VAT where the original lease was VAT-exempt.

A variation to an existing lease is treated as part of the original supply of the lease. Therefore, variations will be exempt unless the landlord has opted to tax the property.

Assignments and reverse assignments

Assignment of a lease where a third party pays a tenant to assign an existing lease is an exempt supply by the tenant subject to the tenant exercising the option to tax.

Lubbock Fine & Co v C & E Commrs (1994)

It was held that the assignment of a lease by a tenant was an exempt supply for VAT purposes.

A reverse assignment occurs where the tenant pays the third party to take the lease from the tenant. This is a standard-rated supply by the third party (assignee).

C & E Commrs v Cantor Fitzgerald International (1999)

The assignor made a payment to Cantor Fitzgerald to induce it to take an assignment of the lease (a reverse assignment). The ECJ held that the relevant supply is a supply of services – agreeing to accept an assignment of a lease of property from a lessee. Such a supply is not the letting of immoveable property as the supplier had no interest in the property at the time of the supply.

2.5.1 Variations to leases

Variations, as with other supplies of land and property, are generally exempt with the option to tax. Customs currently take the view that some variations to leases can be ignored for VAT purposes. A statement of practice was agreed with the Law Society in 1991. This document describes when the variation of a lease does and does not give rise to separate supplies of the surrender of the old lease and the grant of a new one.

2.5.2 Third party costs

If VAT incurred is related to an onward taxable supply it can be recovered in full provided there is a direct and immediate link between the purchase and the onward taxable supply.

C & E Commrs v Redrow Group plc (1999)

Redrow tried to reclaim VAT that it had paid out settling the estate agency fees of prospective purchasers of their new homes. The estate agency fees related to the disposal of the existing homes of the prospective purchasers. Customs argued that there was no direct and immediate link between the sale of the new house and the payment of a third party's estate agency fees.

It was held that Redrow had complete control over the estate agents and invoices were raised to Redrow. Therefore, a 'direct and immediate link' existed and the VAT was recoverable.

Poladon Ltd (1999)

A developer obtained finance to convert a property into residential accommodation. A firm of surveyors were instructed by the bank to monitor the works. The surveyors were paid by the bank. These fees were then charged on to the developer who recovered the VAT. It was held that the services had been supplied to the bank and not the developer so no right to recover VAT arose.

2.5.3   **Service charges**

A service charge levied by a landlord to a tenant follows the VAT liability of the lease concerned. This means the service charge is VAT-exempt if the lease is exempt, but standard-rated if the option to tax has been exercised. Third party service charges are always standard-rated as they are not associated with any interest in land.

Business Enterprises (UK) Ltd (1988)

It was held that cleaning and telephone switchboard services were part of an exempt licence to occupy land and VAT was not therefore reclaimable on related expenditure.

Tower Hamlets Housing Action Trust (2000)

It was held that charges for photocopying services were a separate standard-rated supply whereas the provision of telephones was part of the exempt supply of leased serviced office accommodation. It was held that the photocopying services were not an essential feature of a serviced office whereas the telephone system was an essential feature.

Services provided by a managing agent to a landlord are always standard-rated. The agent may be acting on behalf of the landlord using the landlord's funds in which case the landlord can recover the appropriate VAT, or the agent may re-charge expenses in which case the agent can recover the VAT.

Peter Anthony Estate Ltd (1994)

It was held that an agent who collected rent on behalf of a landlord and kept back a percentage as a fee was liable to VAT on his fee. The exempt land supply was made by the landlord not the rent collecting agent.

Clowance Owners Club Ltd (2002)

It was held that a company who managed and administered timeshare accommodation at a resort was required to register and account for VAT on charges made to timeshare owners. The different charges represented cost components of an overall service of managing timeshare accommodation.

2.6   TRANSFER OF A BUSINESS AS A GOING CONCERN

2.6.1   Generally

If the sale of an investment property is treated as the transfer of a business as a going concern (a TOGC), the supply is neither a supply of goods nor a supply of services to the purchaser. Subject to various conditions, the purchaser is treated as effectively stepping into the shoes of the seller without any VAT consequences.

The TOGC rules are intended to prevent the seller of a business collecting a large sum of VAT, and then absconding with the undeclared VAT, as an illegal 'bonus' payment. The TOGC rules are mandatory and parties to certain transactions must therefore be very careful as incorrect treatment and subsequent rectification can be extremely costly.

The conditions that must be satisfied for a TOGC to exist are the following:

- there must be a going concern to transfer;

- the assets of the business transferred must be used in the same kind of business;

- the purchaser must become a VAT-registered person;

- if only part of business transferred, then that part must be capable of separate operation;

- if the transfer includes property chargeable to VAT because the vendor has opted to tax the rental income, then the purchaser must elect to waive exemption and give written notification of that election to Customs before the 'relevant date' (usually at completion unless a deposit creates an earlier tax point); and

- from 18 March 2004, an additional requirement was introduced as an anti-avoidance measure requiring purchasers of new or opted commercial property to make an additional notification to the vendor. Broadly, the notification is that the purchaser's option to tax will not be disapplied because of the intended future use of the property.

2.6.2 Meaning of 'transfer of a business as a going concern'

Spijkers v Gebroeders Benedik Abattoir (1985)

It was stated that whether a disposal of a business can be classed as a transfer of a going concern and outside the scope of VAT will depend on many factors. Each of these factors will be part of the overall assessment and they cannot be examined independently of each other.

2.6.3 Meaning of 'same kind of business'

Kwik Save Group plc (1994)

Company A contracted to sell property to company B who subsold it to company C. The going concern relief was held not to be available to B.

Zita Modes Sàrl v Administration de l'enregistrement et des domaines (2001)

A company sold the assets of a retail clothing business treating the transaction as a TOGC and not charging VAT. The Luxembourg tax authority issued an assessment charging VAT on the basis that the purchaser was not authorised to trade in the relevant sector. The ECJ held that the transferee must intend to operate the business and not simply liquidate the activity concerned and sell the stock obtained. There was no restriction in the European VAT legislation regarding authorisations to pursue the business activity concerned.

2.6.4 Meaning of 'notifying an election before the relevant date'

Higher Education Statistics Agency Ltd v C & E Commrs (2000)

If land or buildings are purchased at an auction, the relevant date for the option to tax and the transfer of going concern rules is not necessarily the date of the auction. If the auctioneer is acting as an agent of the vendor, the receipt of the deposit by the auctioneer creates the relevant date. If the auctioneer is a stakeholder for the vendor, the relevant date will be when any funds are released to the vendor or the vendor's agent, or completion which ever is earlier.

Chalegrove Properties Ltd (2001)

A company sold a property upon which it had opted to tax. The agreement included a clause stating that the property should be transferred as a going concern and the parties should endeavour to ensure the sale was not treated as a supply for VAT purposes. As part of this process, the purchaser sent a letter notifying Customs of their option to tax on the property. Customs did not receive this letter until after the date of the sale and issued an assessment on the basis that VAT must be accounted for on the sale proceeds. The vendor appealed. The tribunal held that the election was valid as the purchaser had done all they could to notify the election in time and they should not be at the mercy of the postage system in such circumstances.

Trade Only Plant Sales Ltd (2004)

A company purchased a new commercial property. Two years later the company transferred its business to an associated company as a going concern. The property was retained by the original company which then ceased to be VAT-registered. Customs considered that VAT was due on the deemed supply of the property at deregistration as it was less than three years old. Under rules concerning transfers of going concerns, the associated company had to pay the VAT.

3
Residential and charitable property

The basic position for most property transactions, such as the sale or leasing of a building, is that the supply is VAT-exempt resulting in a situation where no VAT on expenditure relating to that property can be recovered.

For commercial property there is the possibility that the person making a supply of the property can 'opt to tax', thereby choosing to account for VAT on the income they receive and recover VAT on purchases made. Alternatively, a transaction may be related to one of the standard-rated exceptions to the exemption.

There are further special rules relating to residential and charitable property which can prove very beneficial both in terms of VAT recovery and on the rates of VAT paid out on services procured.

3.1   RESIDENTIAL DEVELOPMENT LAND

The 'grant of any interest in or right over land or of any licence to occupy land' is exempt from VAT (VAT Act 1994, Schedule 9, Group 1, item 1). In certain instances, a supply of land may be subject to VAT if the option to tax has been exercised by the person supplying the land. This option is, however, disapplied if the land concerned is sold for the purposes of residential development (see Chapter 2). The only exception being where the purchaser of the land intends to sell new dwellings and the vendor and purchaser agree in writing that the option to tax will not be disapplied (VAT Act 1994, Schedule 10, paragraph 2). This allows the vendor to retain the right to recover associated VAT costs.

C & E Commrs v Wiggett Construction (2001)

A company purchased land and was charged VAT. The company recovered the VAT on the basis that they intended to make taxable supplies of new housing. Within six years of this intention being made, the company made an exempt land supply to a housing association as well as concurrently entering into a development contract to carry out construction works on the land. It was held that the VAT recovery should be apportioned between taxable building services and exempt supplies of land.

[The subsequent *Southern Primary Housing* decision has effectively overturned this decision.]

C & E Commrs v Southern Primary Housing Ltd (2004)

A company purchased some land and was charged VAT. The intention was to obtain planning permission for residential development and sell the land to a housing association. The company made a VAT-exempt disposal of the land to the housing association, and also entered into a contract to construct the residential accommodation for the association. The company sought to recover an element of VAT as partly attributable to the taxable supply of construction work. It was held that no VAT recovery was possible as the land purchase was not a 'cost component' of the construction works.

[This decision overturned the *Wiggett* decision above.]

Goldmax Resources Ltd (2001)

A company, in exercising an option, purchased and sold the freehold of an office building on the same day. They had to pay VAT on the purchase price, but the onward sale was exempt as the building was being sold to a housing association. The company reclaimed the VAT on the purchase. The tribunal held that the VAT was not recoverable as there was no taxable onward supply to which the VAT could be attributed.

3.2 THE SALE AND LETTING OF RESIDENTIAL PROPERTY

The first freehold sale or lease of land and buildings can be VAT zero-rated where there is the grant of a 'major interest' by the person constructing or converting the building in one of the following:

(1) a building 'designed as a dwelling or number of dwellings';

(2) a building intended for use solely for a 'relevant residential purpose';

(3) a building intended for use solely for a 'relevant charitable purpose';

(4) a residential building that has been converted from a non-residential building;

(5) a 'substantially reconstructed' protected building; or

(6) an existing residential building that has been derelict for a period in excess of ten years prior to the granting of the 'major interest'.

A grant includes an assignment or surrender.

The zero-rating applies only to the first payment made, for example the initial premium payment, but not any subsequent rental payments which would be exempt from VAT. In the case of shared ownership schemes, where the occupier purchases a proportion of the property and then pays rent to the original owner, the original purchase can be zero-rated by the seller.

Zero-rating for the above property types means that the disposal is a taxable supply with output tax chargeable at 0%. Due to the taxable status of the supply, VAT (input tax) is recoverable by the person making that supply.

3.3 WHAT IS A 'MAJOR INTEREST'?

A 'major interest' is defined in section 96(1) of the VAT Act 1994, as follows:

'"major interest", in relation to land, means the fee simple or a tenancy for a term certain exceeding 21 years, and in relation to Scotland means–

(a) the estate or interest of the proprietor of the dominium utile; or

(b) in the case of land not held on feudal tenure, the estate or interest of the owner, or the lessee's interest under a lease for a period exceeding 21 years'.

Crown copyright material is reproduced with the permission of the Controller of HMSO and the Queen's Printer for Scotland.

A 'fee simple' means in relation to Scotland, the estate or interest of the proprietor of the dominium utile or, in the case of land not held on feudal tenure, the estate or interest of the owner; in relation to Northern Ireland, includes the estate of a person who holds land under a fee farm grant.

C & E Commrs v Briararch (1992)

It was held that a house-builder who constructed houses intended for sale, but then granted short-term VAT-exempt leases before they granted taxable zero-rated 'major interests' in the dwellings were entitled to a degree of VAT recovery. The tribunal held that the house-builder was entitled to recover a proportion of VAT as it always had the intention of selling the dwellings and the lets were a temporary position.

CS & JM Issac (1996)

Zero-rating is only available where there is a grant of a major interest as defined by section 96 of the VAT Act 1994, i.e. a lease in excess of 21 years. In this case, a newly constructed residential apartment was leased for a period of 21 years. Customs contended that VAT could not be recovered on the development costs as there was no grant of a major interest. It was held that a Deed of Rectification issued to alter the residential lease to terms exceeding 21 years in order to make the lease taxable was effective as the intention had always been to make zero-rated supplies.

Stonecliff Caravan Park (1993)

A company constructed 'park homes' on a caravan site and granted pitch agreements. Although it was held that the homes could be buildings designed as dwellings, the pitch agreement was held not to amount to the grant of a major interest in land, but a licence to occupy land, and therefore the onward sale was VAT-exempt preventing recovery of VAT on costs incurred.

Note (13) to Group 5 of Schedule 8 to the VAT Act 1994 states that the grant of an interest in a building designed as a dwelling or number of dwellings (for definition, see Group 5, Note (2) explained in section 3.5 of this text) is not entitled to zero-rated treatment if there is a restriction preventing year-round occupation or use as the grantee's principal private residence.

Livingstone Homes UK Ltd (2000)

It was held in this Scottish case that the sale of holiday dwelling houses were VAT zero-rated as the tribunal considered that the planning conditions did not rule out the use of these holiday properties as a person's principal private residence.

[This decision was considered to be incorrect by the chairman in the subsequent *Loch Tay* tribunal decision.]

Loch Tay Highland Lodges Ltd (2005)

A number of lodges in a holiday development were constructed and then sold. The sales were treated as VAT zero-rated grants of a major interest in a building designed as a dwelling. It was held that due to the restrictions on use in the planning permission, zero-rating was not applicable. The planning restricted use of the lodges to that of holiday accommodation and debarred use as the sole or main residence of the occupants.

[This contrasts with the decision in *Livingstone Homes UK Ltd* (2000).]

3.4 WHO IS THE 'PERSON CONSTRUCTING' THE BUILDING?

The 'person constructing' a building can either be the developer of the building who has constructed or commissioned construction of the building in question, or any contractor or subcontractor who has provided construction services to that developer in constructing that building.

If a development is sold part-completed, then both the persons who started the development and those who completed it will be considered to have 'person constructing' status.

Hulme Trust Educational Foundation Trustees (1978)

It was held that the owner of land which was leased to another for redevelopment was not entitled to recover VAT on the basis that they were a person constructing a building. The owner was not a party to the construction contracts. The words 'person constructing a building' meant either the developer who appointed builders to construct a building or the builder themselves.

Peddars Way Housing Association Ltd (1993)

A housing association sold some dwellings which had been transferred to it by the local authority which had originally constructed them. The housing association claimed 'person constructing' status and sought to zero-rate the sales presumably in order to recover VAT on their costs. The appeal was dismissed. The tribunal stated that there was no mechanism in UK or European law to transfer 'person constructing' status from the council to the housing association.

C & E Commrs v Link Housing Association Ltd (1992)

This case confirmed that it is only the person constructing a building who is entitled to zero-rate his or her supplies of that building. It was also held in this case that the length of time between completion of the construction works and the first supply of a 'major interest' in the property is not relevant in determining eligibility for VAT zero-rating.

Stapenhill Developments Ltd (1984)

The tribunal held that the sale of some development land upon which civil engineering works including piles for foundations had been installed was not a zero-rated supply by 'a person constructing' buildings designed as dwellings. The supply was therefore exempt and consequently no VAT recovery was possible by the company. It was held that there was no specific building on the site to which zero-rating could be attributed.

3.5   **WHAT IS A BUILDING?**

In order for there to be a zero-rated disposal of a residential or charitable building, there is more often than not the requirement that a new building is created. There are specific conditions contained in Notes (16) to (18) to Group 5 of Schedule 8 to the VAT Act 1994 (as amended) that must be satisfied in order for zero-rating to be available.

'(16) For the purpose of this Group, the construction of a building does not include–

(a)   the conversion, reconstruction or alteration of an existing building; or

(b)   any enlargement of, or extension to, an existing building except to the extent the enlargement or extension creates an additional dwelling or dwellings; or

(c)   subject to Note (17) below, the construction of an annexe to an existing building.

(17) Note (16)(c) above shall not apply where the whole or part of an annexe is intended for use solely for a relevant charitable purpose and–

...

(18) A building only ceases to be an existing building when:

(a) demolished completely to ground level; or

(b) the part remaining above ground level consists of no more than a single facade or where a corner site, a double facade, the retention of which is a condition or requirement of statutory planning consent or similar permission.'

Crown copyright material is reproduced with the permission of the Controller of HMSO and the Queen's Printer for Scotland.

Bruce (1991)

A farmer obtained planning permission for 'improvements and extension' to an old farmhouse. Due to the poor condition of the existing building, he had to build a completely new dwelling on the site. Customs would not give a refund of VAT as they considered the works amounted to a reconstruction. The tribunal allowed the farmer's appeal as no part of the original farmhouse remained.

Trident Housing Association Ltd (1992)

The construction of a number of flats on top of a two-storey car park was held to be VAT zero-rated. It was held to be 'wholly inappropriate' to regard the block of flats as an enlargement of the car park.

Midgley (1996)

A dilapidated farmhouse had planning permission for a new extension. In the course of the works it was found necessary to demolish the entire property apart from one wall. Retrospective planning permission was granted for the scheme as built. It was held that the building had ceased to be an existing building for VAT purposes and that the construction works could be VAT zero-rated.

Evans (2001)

The appellant considered that he had constructed a new dwelling even though a single façade wall of a previous construction was incorporated in the new building. The retention of the original wall was not a requirement of planning consent for the building. The tribunal ruled that the work should be standard-rated as there was an existing building on the site.

Naylor (2001)

It was held that a planning permission that referred to front, side and rear extensions and new roof could amount to a requirement to retain a single façade and hence the subsequent construction of a building qualified for a DIY builders refund as a new build dwelling.

Cantrell (t/a Foxearth Lodge Nursing Home) v C & E Commrs (2003)

The construction of a self-contained extension to an existing nursing home was held to be VAT zero-rated and not an annexe to any existing building.

Menzies (1997)

The construction of a new residential building one metre away from an existing building in the grounds of a field centre was held to be VAT zero-rated as a building designed for use solely for a relevant residential purpose. The construction of a link between the two buildings 28 days later did not change the nature of the project to an alteration of an existing building.

3.6 **WHAT IS A BUILDING 'DESIGNED AS A DWELLING'?**

Note (2) to Group 5 of Schedule 8 to the VAT Act 1994 defined a building designed as a dwelling in the following terms:

'(2) A building is designed as a dwelling or a number of dwellings where, in relation to each dwelling, the following conditions are satisfied:

(a) the dwelling consists of self-contained living accommodation;

(b) there is no provision for direct internal access from the dwelling to any other dwelling or part of a dwelling;

(c) the separate use or disposal of the dwelling is not prohibited by the terms of any covenant, statutory planning consent or similar provision; and

(d) statutory planning consent has been granted in respect of that dwelling and its construction or conversion has been carried out in accordance with that consent.'

Crown copyright material is reproduced with the permission of the Controller of HMSO and the Queen's Printer for Scotland.

The above conditions for a building 'designed as a dwelling' should be distinguished from the currently generally accepted definition of a dwelling as formulated in *Uratemp Ventures Ltd v Collins* (2001) (of relevance where it is necessary to establish where a building is non-residential) and a 'single household dwelling' (which applies with regard to the application of the 5% VAT rate for the provision of certain construction services).

The test as to what constitutes self-contained living accommodation as required by Note (2)(a) above has evolved over the last ten years with the *Uratemp* decision providing the most current accepted definition for a dwelling.

Uratemp Ventures Ltd v Collins (2001)

In a case regarding an assured tenancy under the *Housing Act* 1988, a hotel room with no cooking facilities beyond that of a plug was a dwelling. It was held that residential accommodation was a dwelling if it was the occupier's home, where they lived, returned to and which formed the centre of their existence.

University of Bath (1995)

A university which had constructed some buildings and used them for student accommodation and also for vacation lettings for non-educational purposes carried out a refurbishment of the buildings concerned. The buildings comprised a number of separate 'apartments' – each comprised a number of study bedrooms with en suite facilities and communal kitchen facilities. The tribunal held that the buildings were not 'designed as a dwelling or number of dwellings' and were not 'intended for use solely for a relevant residential or a relevant charitable purpose'.

The *University of Bath* decision may well have been decided differently today as a result of the *Uratemp* decision.

Agudas Israel Housing Association Ltd (2003)

A housing association constructed an additional floor on top of a two-storey care home. The new accommodation comprised eight self-contained bed-sitting rooms each with an en suite shower room. It was held that the works qualified for VAT zero-rating. This case confirmed that residential accommodation with limited cooking facilities could be seen to be self-contained. The *Uratemp* decision was held to be relevant in determining what comprised 'self-contained living accommodation' under Note (2)(a).

Oldrings Development Kingsclere Ltd (2000)

The construction of a single-storey self-contained building in the grounds of another dwelling was held to qualify for VAT zero-rating as it satisfied all the conditions to qualify as a building designed as a dwelling. It was not relevant that its use was primarily as a painting studio for the owner's wife.

Wiseman (2001)

It was held that a residential building which was incapable either of separate use or of separate disposal was excluded from zero-rating – both conditions had to be satisfied (VAT Act 1994, Schedule 8, Group 5, Note (2)(c)).

Davison (2000)

It was held that residential accommodation provided above a garage did not qualify for VAT zero-rating as it had not been constructed in accordance with the statutory planning consent granted and therefore Note (2)(d) to Group 5 of Schedule 8 to the VAT Act 1994 was not satisfied.

A recent trend is the construction of live work units. These are buildings or parts of buildings designed for occupation for both living and work purposes. The work area may be a discrete area within the accommodation or it may not have specific identifiable boundaries.

Where there is a discrete area the commercial element must be separated from the living area and treated according to the rules for non-residential property. Any occupational restriction does not deny zero-rating being available for the supply of construction services where all other conditions of Note (2) to Group 5 are satisfied.

Garages

Note (3) to Group 5 states that a garage constructed at the same time as the construction of a new dwelling that is intended to be occupied with that dwelling can also be zero-rated.

3.7   **WHAT IS A 'NON-RESIDENTIAL' BUILDING?**

A non-residential building is defined in Note (7) to Group 5 of Schedule 8 to the VAT Act 1994 (as amended), as follows:

'(7) A building or part of a building is 'non-residential' if–

(a)   it is neither designed, nor adapted, for use–

(i)   as a dwelling or number of dwellings, or

(ii)   for a relevant residential purpose; or

(b) it is designed, or adapted, for such use but–

(i) it was constructed more than ten years before the grant of the major interest; and

(ii) no part of it has, in the period of ten years immediately preceding the grant, been used as a dwelling or for a relevant residential purpose.'

Crown copyright material is reproduced with the permission of the Controller of HMSO and the Queen's Printer for Scotland.

The grant of a major interest in a building converted from non-residential accommodation to a building designed as a dwelling or number of dwellings qualifies for VAT zero-rating, thus allowing recovery of the VAT incurred on conversion and sale costs.

The definition of 'non-residential' (VAT Act 1994, Schedule 8, Group 5, Note (7)) should be distinguished from the conditions for a 'building designed as a dwelling or number of dwellings (VAT Act 1994, Schedule 8, Group 5, Note (2)). The current interpretation of 'non-residential' relies on the wider definition of a dwelling as advanced in the *Uratemp Ventures Ltd v Collins* (2001) case rather than the various conditions in Note (2) above which relate to the formation and disposal of new dwellings.

Temple House Developments Ltd (1997)

A company purchased a public house and obtained planning permission for its conversion into two semi-detached dwellings. It reclaimed the VAT on the purchase and subsequent conversion costs. Customs issued assessments to recover the tax. The company appealed, arguing that the public house had been a 'non-residential building' as defined in VAT law so that the subsequent sales would be zero-rated supplies and the input tax was recoverable. The tribunal accepted this contention and allowed the appeal, holding that no part of the public house 'was designed as a dwelling' before the conversion.

[This tribunal has subsequently been considered to be incorrect. See *Tobell* below.]

Tobell (1998)

An individual bought and converted a pub into a dwelling for his own occupation. He claimed the VAT under the self build VAT reclaim rules on the basis he had completed a residential conversion. Customs refused the reclaim on the basis that the building already contained residential accommodation at upper floor level. The tribunal declined to follow the *Temple House* decision on the grounds that the definition of non-residential was a different test to that for the creation of a new dwelling under Notes (7) and (2) respectively of Group 5 of Schedule 8 to the VAT Act 1994.

Look Ahead Housing and Care Ltd (2000)

This case concerned the conversion by a housing association of bed-sits into self-contained flats. It was held that the bed-sits were 'non-residential' and that the conversion works could therefore be VAT zero-rated.

[The arguments in this case have since been dismissed in the more recent *Amicus* (2002) tribunal due to the adoption of the *Uratemp Ventures Ltd v Collins (2001)* decision as authority for the definition of a dwelling. This tribunal is overturned by subsequent tribunals.]

Calam Vale Ltd (2000)

This case concerned the sale of two dwellings following the vertical conversion of a public house into two self-contained dwellings. It was held that the sale of the dwellings was VAT-exempt, as each new dwelling contained part of the existing first-floor living accommodation, and the rules for zero-rating the sale were not therefore satisfied. VAT incurred on the conversion was thus not recoverable. The tribunal followed a two-stage test to determine whether a qualifying conversion had occurred. The rules are as follows: the end-product must be a 'dwelling' as defined in the VAT legislation; and the preconversion status must satisfy the VAT definition of 'non-residential'.

Amicus Group Ltd (2002)

It was held that the conversion of bed-sits into self-contained flats did not give rise to VAT zero-rated conversion services for a housing association. The existing bed-sits in this case were classed as being 'residential' and therefore no conversion took place for VAT purposes.

[This case reverses the decision in *Look Ahead Housing Association* (2000), due to reference to a recent non-VAT case concerning the definition of a 'dwelling' (*Uratemp Ventures Ltd v Collins* (2001)).]

Kingscastle Ltd (2002)

Part of the conversion of the upper floors of a pub into separate flats was considered to be attributable to an exempt final sale, rather than a zero-rated sale, thus debarring recovery of VAT for Kingscastle Ltd, where the works related to existing 'residential' accommodation previously used by the publican, rather than 'non-residential' usage.

[This decision was in line with the arguments stated in the *Amicus* tribunal.]

Note (9) to Group 5 of Schedule 8 to the VAT Act 1994 states that the zero-rating can still apply to the sale of a residential conversion, even where the building converted already contains residential parts, as long as the result of that conversion is to create an additional dwelling or dwellings.

C & E Commrs v Jacobs (2004)

A boarding school was converted by a private individual into a large house with three self-contained staff flats. The owner claimed a refund of VAT on the conversion work.

Customs rejected the claim on the basis that the building had previously been used for residential purposes, so that the work did not qualify for zero-rating. The High Court accepted that the conversion had created three additional dwellings and therefore qualified for zero-rating under the criteria included within Note (9).

Belvedere Properties (Cheltenham) Ltd (2004)

A company reclaimed input tax on the conversion of a property, which had originally been used as a commercial property but had subsequently been used as bed-sitting accommodation, into nine self-contained flats. The commissioners rejected the claim and the company appealed, contending that the work was a residential conversion so that the sale of the property qualified for zero-rating. The tribunal rejected this contention and dismissed the appeal, holding that the property had been used as a 'dwelling' before the conversion, so that the work failed to qualify for zero-rating.

3.8 WHAT IS A BUILDING USED FOR A 'RELEVANT RESIDENTIAL PURPOSE'?

The VAT Act 1994 (as amended), Schedule 8, Group 5, Note (4) defines 'relevant residential purpose' as follows:

'(4) Use for a relevant residential purpose means use as–

(a) a home or other institution providing residential accommodation for children;

(b) a home or other institution providing residential accommodation with personal care for persons in need of personal care by reason of old age, disablement, past or present dependence on alcohol or drugs or past or present mental disorder;

(c) a hospice;

(d) residential accommodation for students or school pupils;

(e) residential accommodation for members of any of the armed forces;

(f)   a monastery, nunnery or similar establishment; or

(g)   an institution which is the sole or main residence of at least 90 per cent of its residents,

except use as a hospital, prison or similar institution or an hotel, inn or similar establishment.'

Crown copyright material is reproduced with the permission of the Controller of HMSO and the Queen's Printer for Scotland.

Broadly, a building used for a 'relevant residential purpose' will be both residential in nature and have some element of communal facilities shared between residents, such as cooking and dining facilities. It could also include, for example, a warden's office, launderettes and communal living rooms. A qualifying use certificate must be completed confirming the intended use of the building 'solely' for 'relevant residential purposes'.

Urdd Gobaith Cymru (1997)

It was held that the minimum length of stay at an institution for Welsh language students was not relevant in determining whether the building was used solely for 'relevant residential purposes'. The restrictions in the VAT legislation only related to the type of persons staying in the building and not to the length of their stay.

Denman College (1998)

It was held that the accommodation, which did not include catering or kitchen facilities and was intended for use by short-stay students attending courses which lasted between three and six days, were buildings used 'solely for a relevant residential purpose'.

General Healthcare Group Ltd (2001)

A building which was used as a rehabilitation home for people who had suffered brain injuries was held to be used 'solely for a relevant residential purpose' on the basis it was a home or institution providing residential accommodation.

It was not used as 'a hospital ... or similar institution' as suggested by Customs. The occupants who stayed an average time in excess of two years did receive care but they did not receive any medical treatment or diagnosis at the premises.

Wallis Ltd (2003)

A residential building for people who were mentally ill was held to be used as a 'hospital or similar institution' and was therefore excluded from zero-rating.

3.9 WHAT IS A BUILDING USED FOR A 'RELEVANT CHARITABLE PURPOSE'?

Relevant charitable purpose is defined in the VAT Act 1994 (as amended), Schedule 8, Group 5, Note (6) as follows:

'(6) Use for a relevant charitable purpose means use by a charity in either or both the following ways, namely–

(a) otherwise than in the course or furtherance of a business;

(b) as a village hall or similarly in providing social or recreational facilities for a local community.'

Crown copyright material is reproduced with the permission of the Controller of HMSO and the Queen's Printer for Scotland.

A qualifying use certificate must be completed confirming the intended use of the building 'solely' for 'relevant charitable purposes'.

A building is not used 'solely' for a qualifying purpose when it is used at the same time for other purposes; used at a different time for other purposes; or never used for qualifying purposes. It is, however, possible by concession to ignore minor non-qualifying use. In general, a minor non-qualifying use is any use less than 10% of the total, whether based on a calculation of the time available for use, by areas or by head count. It is necessary to disclose the calculations to Customs in connection with any non-qualifying use that is considered to be minor.

Note (6)(a) requires the activities carried out in any building concerned to be non-business. The mere confirmation of charitable status alone does not qualify for non-business status. It is necessary to analyse the nature of the activities proposed or carried out in the building concerned. If the charity does something for which it receives payment, it is generally considered to be in business. The failure to make any profit is not relevant.

Some activities are always deemed to be 'business'. These include the provision of membership benefits by clubs, associations and similar bodies in return for a subscription or other consideration and admission to premises for a charge.

C & E Commrs v Morrison's Academy Boarding Houses Association (1978)

This case concerned a private school registered as a charity which had established a company to charge for boarding fees. The school argued that as a charity it was not a business. It was held that a charity could be in business, as supplies could be made for a consideration. Profit was not deemed a necessity to have a business.

C & E Commrs v Yarburgh Children's Trust (2001)

The High Court upheld the tribunal's decision that a newly constructed building leased to a play group qualified as a 'relevant charitable purpose' building, as it was designed for non-business educational purposes.

C & E Commrs v St Paul's Community Project Ltd (2004)

A charity commissioned the construction of a new building that was to be used as a nursery. The charity claimed that VAT zero-rating applied to the construction of this building. Customs rejected the claim on the basis that the nursery was a business. The Chancery Division upheld the tribunal's decision that the nursery was operating on a non-business basis for VAT purposes.

Note (6)(b) to Group 5 of Schedule 8 to the VAT Act 1994 provides a second opportunity for zero-rating village halls, church halls, sports halls and community centres used by charities to provide social or recreational facilities for the local community. Business use in these circumstances does not deny the zero-rating.

Jubilee Hall Recreation Centre v C & E Commrs (1999)

Jubilee Hall was a charity-run sports and fitness centre located in a listed building. Various alterations, for which zero-rating was claimed, occurred. It was held that zero-rating did not apply as the centre was not owned, organised and administered by the local community for the local community and therefore did not qualify as a 'relevant charitable purpose' building for VAT purposes.

South Aston Community Association; IB Construction Ltd (2002)

An association formed to 'promote health and welfare and to advance the education and training of the community' constructed a new community centre and claimed zero-rating for the works for the construction of a 'relevant charitable purpose' building. Customs disagreed, ruling that the works were VAT standard-rated. The tribunal agreed with Customs. As the building was used partly by a local college for business purposes and use was not restricted to the local community, the conditions for zero-rating were not satisfied.

League of Friends of Kingston Hospital (1994)

The construction of a building housing a scanner was held not to be a 'relevant charitable purpose' building and therefore zero-rating was deemed not applicable. It was held that the building was used for 'business' purposes by the adjacent hospital. The fact that the works were paid for by a charity was irrelevant in this case.

3.9.1 Charitable annexe

Notes (16) and (17) to Group 5 of Schedule 8 to the VAT Act 1994 provide that zero-rating is capable of applying to the supply by a person constructing, or to services in the course of construction, of an annexe used solely for a relevant charitable purpose. The legislation anticipates that the annexe is likely to be attached and linked to an existing building. Confirmation and certification of qualifying use would be required.

Note (17) states that the annexe must be capable of functioning independently from the existing building to which it is linked and that the main access to the annexe is not via the existing building nor that the main access to the existing building is via the annexe.

In the case of the construction of an annexe building, a number of factors should be considered:

• the annexe must be capable of functioning independently from the existing building to which it is attached. This could be indicated by dedicated services capable of separate operation from the adjacent building;

• the annexe should not merely be an extension or enlargement of an existing building. Any major degree of integration into the existing building would not be considered to be an annexe; and

• where only part of the annexe is used for qualifying 'relevant charitable purposes', an apportionment must be made between construction works to the zero-rated portion and the VAT standard-rated portion.

Grace Baptist Church (1998)

A new annexe was constructed at a church to replace its existing chapel house. It was held that the construction works qualified for zero-rating as an annexe under Note (17) rather than as an extension under Note (16).

Castle Caereinion Recreation Association (2002)

Two additional rooms were added to a village hall. It was accepted that the rooms would be used for 'relevant charitable purposes'. The tribunal held that one room qualified as an annexe and could be zero-rated whilst the other was an extension and was therefore VAT standard-rated.

Macnamara (1999)

The construction of a two-storey 'extension' at a school was denied treatment as a VAT zero-rated annexe used for a 'relevant charitable purpose' on the grounds that the degree of integration between the new and existing building was such as to make it an 'extension' rather than an annexe building. In addition, the new building was deemed to be 'not capable of functioning independently from the existing building', as required by the VAT legislation.

Shiri Guru Nanaka Sikh Temple (1996)

An extension or annexe was constructed at a Sikh Temple. The works being intended to create a space intended for use solely for a relevant charitable purpose. It was held that the works were standard-rated as the entrance for the new area was via the existing building and hence it failed the specific requirements of the legislation.

Woodley Baptist Church (2001)

A Baptist Church arranged for the construction of a youth centre, above the church hall at the rear of the church, with a separate entrance. The commissioners issued a ruling that the work was standard-rated. The Church appealed, contending that the work should be treated as a zero-rated annexe within Group 5, Note (17). The tribunal rejected this contention and dismissed the appeal, holding on the evidence that the work was an extension rather than an annexe.

3.10 WHAT IS A 'SUBSTANTIALLY RECONSTRUCTED PROTECTED BUILDING'?

3.10.1 Protected building

The term 'protected building' is defined in the VAT Act 1994 (Schedule 8, Group 6, Note (1)), as follows:

'(1) "Protected building" means a building which is designed to remain as or become a dwelling or number of dwellings ... or is intended for use solely for a relevant residential purpose or a relevant charitable purpose after the reconstruction or alteration and which, in either case, is–

(a) a listed building, within the meaning of–

   (i)   the Planning (Listed Buildings and Conservation Areas) Act 1990; or

   (ii) the Planning (Listed Buildings and Conservation Areas) (Scotland) Act 1997; or

   (iii) the Planning (Northern Ireland) Order 1991; or

(b) a scheduled monument, within the meaning of–

   (i)   the Ancient Monuments and Archaeological Areas Act 1979; or

   (ii) the Historic Monuments and Archaeological Objects (Northern Ireland) Order 1995.'

Crown copyright material is reproduced with the permission of the Controller of HMSO and the Queen's Printer for Scotland.

Broadly speaking, a 'protected building' is a building that is either a listed building or scheduled monument and that is designed to remain as or become a dwelling or number of dwellings, or a building that is intended for use for a 'relevant residential or charitable purpose'.

3.10.2 Substantially reconstructed

The term 'substantially reconstructed' is defined in the Note (4) to Group 6 of Schedule 8 to the VAT Act 1994 (as amended) as follows:

'(4) For the purposes of item 1, a protected building shall not be regarded as substantially reconstructed unless the reconstruction is such that at least one of the following conditions is fulfilled when the reconstruction is completed–

(a) that, of the works carried out to effect the reconstruction, at least three-fifths, measured by reference to cost, are of such a nature that the supply of services (other than excluded services), materials and other items to carry out the works, would, if supplied by a taxable person, be within either item 2 or item 3 of this Group; and

(b) that the reconstructed building incorporates no more of the original building (that is to say, the building as it was before the reconstruction began) than the external walls, together with other external features of architectural or historic interest;

and in paragraph (a) above "excluded services" means the services of an architect, surveyor or other person acting as consultant or in a supervisory capacity.'

Crown copyright material is reproduced with the permission of the Controller of HMSO and the Queen's Printer for Scotland.

Where a protected building is 'substantially reconstructed', the freehold sale or grant of a lease in excess of 21 years can be zero-rated.

A protected building is 'substantially reconstructed' if, in addition to the ordinary meaning of the term, either:

• at least 60% of the reconstruction work (measured by reference to cost) would qualify for zero-rating as approved alterations if supplied by a builder who is a taxable person; or

• the reconstructed building incorporates no part of the original building other than the external walls and any other external features of architectural or historic interest.

Certification will be required in order for the sale to be VAT zero-rated in the case of buildings to be used for 'relevant residential' or 'relevant charitable purposes'.

Lordsregal Ltd (2004)

The company reclaimed input tax on the basis that it had carried out a 'substantial reconstruction' of a listed property, so that the sale would be zero-rated. Customs rejected the claim on the basis that the work did not amount to a 'substantial reconstruction', so that the sale of the building would be exempt and VAT not recoverable. Lordsregal Ltd appealed. The VAT tribunal allowed the appeal, finding that when the company purchased the building, it was 'a ruin, unfit for habitation despite the vendor remaining in occupation'.

3.11 CHANGE OF QUALIFYING USE

Where a building is used for non-qualifying purposes within ten years of the issue of a qualifying use certificate there will be a clawback of VAT (VAT Act 1994, Schedule 10, paragraph 1).

This clawback provision which applies to relevant residential use and relevant charitable use buildings may be triggered if the building concerned is either sold or let to someone who uses it for non-qualifying purposes, or it is used by the recipient of the original zero-rated supply for non-qualifying purposes.

If the building is sold or leased to some one for non-qualifying purposes VAT must be charged on the sale. If it is used by the issuer of the original qualifying use certificate for non-qualifying purposes then a self-supply charge will arise and VAT will become due based on the extent of non-qualifying use and the number of years of previous qualifying use.

These rules do not apply to dwellings or situations where zero-rated supplies related to approved alterations to a protected building have occurred.

4
Construction services

Construction services are VAT standard-rated at 17.5% unless they can be treated at either the zero or 5% rate of VAT.

4.1 NEW BUILDINGS

The provision of construction services and goods is generally VAT standard-rated at 17.5%. There is however, a zero rate of VAT available for services provided in the course of construction of certain new buildings (VAT Act 1994, Schedule 8, Group 5, item 2). The buildings include:

- a building 'designed as a dwelling' or a number of dwellings;

- a building that will be used solely for a 'relevant residential purpose';

- a building that will be used solely for a 'relevant charitable purpose'; and

- any civil engineering work necessary for the development of a permanent park for residential caravans.

The services of an architect, surveyor or any person acting in a supervisory capacity are always VAT standard-rated at 17.5%.

A qualifying use certificate is required from the owner of any 'relevant residential purpose' or 'relevant charitable purpose' building, and should be handed to the contractors undertaking the construction works.

Chapter 3 examines in detail the case law in association with the definition of a building, a building designed as a dwelling or number of dwellings, a building that will be used solely for a 'relevant residential purpose', and a building that will be used solely for a 'relevant charitable purpose'.

4.2 WORKS 'IN THE COURSE OF CONSTRUCTION'

Only construction works carried out 'in the course of construction' of a new building can be VAT zero-rated.

Broadly, works are carried out 'in the course of construction' of a building if they take place prior to completion or are related to snagging duties. This also includes any works that are closely related to the construction of the building such as:

- the demolition of pre-existing structures, ground works, main services, landscaping, access and drainage;

- the demolition of existing buildings or structures to allow construction to commence – this would not always be the case where the demolition works were carried out as a separate contract prior to the letting of the main building contract;

- the provision of ground works to prepare the site for new construction works, but not including site investigations carried out prior to the letting of the main contract;

- the provision of mains water and electricity;

- the provision of access to the building by means of paths, roads, drives, and so on;

- the provision of site walls and soft landscaping works such as turfing as required by planning consents for a scheme.

The construction of tennis courts, swimming pools, and ornamental works such as fishponds and rockeries, in the grounds of a dwelling cannot be VAT zero-rated.

Any goods that are hired in the course of construction work will be VAT standard-rated. This includes items such as scaffolding (but see the *GT Scaffolding* case on page 131), the hire of mobile offices, and plant and machinery. These items may be subsumed into a larger onward supply of construction services and thereby be classified at a lower or zero rate of VAT where applicable.

University of Hull (1975)

It was held that a building remains in the course of construction until the external envelope is sealed and all essential services such as plumbing and electrical systems have been installed. Fitting out and furnishing was considered not to be in the course of construction.

McElroy (1977)

An individual purchased and finished off the construction of a partly completed house from a developer whose builder had gone bankrupt. The shell of the building was complete and the individual completed the internal fit out and decoration. The individual applied for a DIY house-builder's VAT refund. Customs considered the building he purchased had already been completed. The individual appealed and the tribunal allowed the appeal. It was held that more than one person was capable of having 'person constructing' status and that completion of the works meant completion to a habitable state.

Lambert's Construction Ltd (1992)

The tribunal chairman stated that 'in the course of construction' covered the entire period from the commencement of work on a site until the dwelling is completed.

C & E Commrs v Rannoch School Ltd (1993)

Civil engineering work carried out before a new dwelling or new qualifying building can be occupied can be zero-rated as part of the services provided 'in the course of construction' of such a building. This case concerned the installation of a sewage treatment plant in association with the construction of a new boarding house.

C & E Commrs v St Mary's Roman Catholic High School (1996)

This case considered the extent of a 'building'. It was held that those parts not being part of the building but being required for its efficient and lawful use were part of the building for VAT purposes (a school playground in association with a school building in this case). The term 'in the course of construction' was also considered and it was held that a 13-year break between the main construction works and other additional works was too long to allow the later works to be included as part of the main zero-rated works.

Dart Major Works Ltd (2004)

A listed dwelling was severely damaged in a fire. Some demolition works were instructed immediately after the fire on safety grounds and then later in preparation for the construction of a replacement dwelling. The tribunal held that the demolition services were both related to the zero-rated construction for a new dwelling and also in the course of construction of the new dwelling, and as such could be zero-rated themselves. There was no delay between the demolition and the process of constructing the new dwelling.

JM Associates (2002)

The construction of conservatories for the owners of newly constructed houses was held to be VAT standard-rated. The tribunal concluded that the conservatory was an extension or enlargement as the house was no longer in the course of construction.

Gilbourne (1974)

It was held that the services of designing, erecting and striking scaffolding was zero-rated in connection with the construction of a new house, but that the hire was VAT standard-rated.

GT Scaffolding Ltd (2003)

It was held that the supply of scaffolding services could be VAT zero-rated as services provided in the course of construction of new dwellings rather than a hire of scaffold. Due to the more stringent regulations and requirements for erecting and adapting access scaffolding, the company retained the legal possession of the scaffolding throughout the duration of the contract.

R & M Scaffolding Ltd (2004)

It was held that the erection and dismantling of scaffolding in the course of construction of houses was zero-rated. However, once the scaffold was erected and certified as safe, possession passed to its customer and reverted to a hire agreement which was VAT standard-rated.

ME Smith (Electrical Engineers) Ltd (1994)

The tribunal held that zero-rating could not apply to the services of an electrical subcontractor as his supplies had been to the main contractor rather than the owner of the 'relevant charitable purpose' building concerned.

The construction or conversion of an existing building to form a garage can be VAT zero-rated, if constructed at the same time as a new dwelling or dwellings.

Chipping Sodbury Town Trust (1999)

The construction of two garages four months after the issuing of the certificate of practical completion was VAT standard-rated. The garages were not constructed in the course of constructing the new dwellings.

Simister (1993)

The conservatory and various fittings were held not to have been installed in the course of construction of a new dwelling. These items had been the subject of a DIY house-builder's VAT claim after having been purchased following the acquisition of a newly built house.

4.3   BUILDING MATERIALS

The supply of building materials is VAT standard-rated at 17.5%. Item 4 of Group 5 of Schedule 8 to the VAT Act 1994 provides that the supply of building materials to a person to whom the supplier is also providing construction services, where these materials are incorporated into the building or its site, can be zero-rated.

The supply of building materials installed in conjunction with reduced-rate building services will also attract the reduced rate, provided that they are supplied by the person installing them and the installation services qualify for the reduced rate.

Building materials are defined in Note (22) to Group 5, as goods of a description ordinarily incorporated by builders in a building of that description (or its site), but not including:

- finished or prefabricated furniture, other than furniture designed to be fitted in kitchens;

- materials for the construction of fitted furniture, other than kitchen furniture;

- electrical or gas appliances, unless the appliance is an appliance that is:

    - designed to heat space or water (or both) or to provide ventilation, air cooling, air purification, or dust extraction; or

    - intended for use in a building designed as a number of dwellings and is a door-entry system, a waste disposal unit or a machine for compacting waste; or

    - a burglar alarm, a fire alarm, or fire safety equipment, or designed solely for the purpose of enabling aid to be summoned in an emergency; or

    - a lift or hoist;

- carpets or carpeting material.

C & E Commrs v McLean Homes Midland Ltd (1993)

This case considered whether wardrobes installed in newly constructed dwellings could be VAT zero-rated or should be VAT standard-rated as 'fitted furniture'. It was held that the VAT liability depended on the degree of integration into the building.

Edmond Homes Ltd (1994)

It was held that a speculative house-builder was able to recover VAT incurred on a vanity unit, as the unit in question was installed to support the wash-hand basin and to hide pipe work, rather than as an item of prefabricated or finished furniture. VAT recovery is specifically denied in relation to prefabricated or finished furniture unless it is kitchen furniture.

Wade (1994)

The tribunal held that wardrobes not predominantly formed from the structure of the dwelling in which they stood were not capable of being VAT zero-rated and were therefore VAT standard-rated.

Moores Furniture Group Ltd (1997)

Wardrobes formed by fixing shelves and a set of doors across the front of a recess which formed part of the fabric of a dwelling were held to qualify for VAT zero-rating. Wardrobes with plinths or end panels are classed as furniture and thus VAT standard-rated.

Birmingham Council for Old People (1996)

Lockers installed in a recently completed nursing home were held not to have been installed 'in the course of construction' of the building and were also held to be 'furniture' rather than 'building materials' for VAT purposes, thus the works were excluded from the zero-rating relief.

Sheldon School (1998)

A grant maintained school fitted out a science block with a series of bollards (some housing sink, taps and gas; others housing electrical and gas supplies) between which moveable tables were positioned. The tribunal held that the bollards, although fixed to the floor, were 'finished or prefabricated furniture' within Note (22) to Group 5 and therefore did not qualify for zero-rating.

Erinmore Homes Ltd (2001)

Integrated electric ovens and hobs were held not to be items upon which a house-builder could recover VAT.

McCarthy (t/a Croft Homes) (2000)

Electrically operated security gates were held to be VAT standard-rated when supplied in connection with new dwellings. They did not qualify for zero-rating since they were not items ordinarily incorporated by builders and they were also electrical appliances. Therefore, they were excluded by the VAT legislation.

C & E Commrs v Jeffs (t/a J & J Joinery) (1995)

A joinery partnership supplied various items of joinery on a zero-rated basis to the owners of a listed dwelling. It was held that the zero rate could not apply as there was a dominant supply of goods and the only services provided were the basic obligations imposed on any person selling goods. Zero-rating is only available for supplies of services.

2S Airchangers Ltd (1994)

Mechanical ventilation systems with heat recovery can be treated as zero-rated where installed as part of qualifying works to dwellings. It was held that the systems were building materials and were 'articles of a kind ordinarily installed by builders'.

Rialto Homes plc (1999)

The planting of shrubs and trees which were part of a scheme for soft and hard landscaping approved by the planning authority were held to be goods ordinarily incorporated in association with new dwellings and could therefore be VAT zero-rated. The tribunal accepted this contention and allowed the appeal.

McCarthy & Stone plc (1992)

Carpeting materials cannot be subject to reduced or zero rates of VAT.

4.4 CONSTRUCTION SERVICES TO EXISTING BUILDINGS

4.4.1 Housing association conversions

Item 3 of Group 5 of Schedule 8 to the VAT Act 1994 allows zero-rating to apply to the conversion of a 'non-residential' building by a 'relevant housing association' into a building designed as a dwelling or number of dwellings or a building intended for use solely for a relevant residential purpose. The services of an architect, surveyor or any person acting as a consultant or in a supervisory capacity are specifically excluded.

These works can include the construction or conversion of a non-residential building to form a garage, so long as the work is carried out at the same time as the main conversion and the garage is intended to be occupied with the converted dwellings.

A 'relevant housing association' is defined at Note (21) to Group 5 of Schedule 8 to the Act (as amended), as follows:

'(21) In Item 3 "relevant housing association" means–

(a) a registered social landlord within the meaning of Part 1 of the Housing Act 1996,

(b) a registered housing association within the meaning of the Housing Associations Act 1985 (Scottish registered housing associations), or

(c) a registered housing association within the meaning of Part II of the Housing (Northern Ireland) Order 1992 (Northern Irish registered housing association).'

Crown copyright material is reproduced with the permission of the Controller of HMSO and the Queen's Printer for Scotland.

4.4.2 Approved alterations to protected buildings

Item 2 of Group 6 of Schedule 8 to the VAT Act 1994 provides that any services provided in the course of an approved alteration to a protected building can be VAT zero-rated. Repair and maintenance works and the services of an architect, surveyor or any person acting as a consultant or in a supervisory capacity are specifically excluded.

4.4.2.1 Protected buildings

Broadly speaking, a protected building is either a building designed as a dwelling or a building intended solely for use for a 'relevant residential purpose' or 'relevant charitable purpose', and is either a listed building or a scheduled monument.

There are three classes of listed building in England and Wales: Grade I, Grade II* and Grade II. In Scotland, the classes are Grade A, Grade B and Grade C(S). Northern Ireland does not have a grading system.

For the purposes of the VAT legislation, a protected building does not include those buildings that are unlisted but situated in a conservation area, or those included in non-statutory local lists.

Scheduled monuments are usually archaeological sites, ruined buildings or early industrial structures included in a statutory schedule of sites of national importance.

C & E Commrs v Zielinski Baker & Partners Ltd (2004)

The House of Lords held that alterations to some outbuildings to provide a swimming pool and games room to a listed house were not eligible for zero-rating, as the outbuildings were not classed as part of the 'protected building'.

4.4.2.2 Approved alterations

Note (6) to Group 6 of Schedule 8 to the VAT Act 1994 provides that an 'approved alteration' means works of alteration for which the relevant consents required have been obtained, but does not include any works of repair or maintenance, or any incidental alteration to the fabric of a building which results from the carrying out of repairs or maintenance work. The relevant consents defined by the legislation are listed building consent or equivalent statutory processes where scheduled monuments or buildings on Crown, Duchy or Church land are concerned.

Listed building consent is required for alterations to listed buildings which affect the architectural or historic character of the building concerned. This consent applies to the entirety of the exterior and interior of the building. Other consents have similar criteria although the details of the application process will be different.

4.4.2.3 Crown or Duchy buildings

If there is a Crown or Duchy interest in a building, the department concerned will follow a non-statutory planning procedure with its own particular documentation. It will be necessary to examine the documents to determine whether listed building consent would ordinarily have been necessary under the normal planning rules. If so, the building concerned can be treated as a protected building. The non-statutory procedure therefore replaces the need for listed building consent.

Evans (1989)

An approved alteration is an alteration to a protected building that both required and has obtained listed building consent or scheduled monument consent. It was held in that Customs are not bound by the views of the planning authority as to which works require consent. In addition, the consent must be granted before commencement of the works.

Dart Major Works Ltd (2004)

A listed dwelling was damaged in a fire and required demolition. It was held that the works were not 'approved alterations' as the consent was not granted until after the works had commenced. The works were, however, still zero-rated as part of the construction of a new dwelling.

Adams (2003)

Underpinning works and a replacement retaining wall were held to be VAT zero-rated as approved alterations to a protected building that was slipping down a hillside.

All Saints with St Nicholas Church (1999)

The tribunal held that a new lighting system and rewiring installation formed part of the fabric of a listed church and was therefore approved alterations to a protected building. Zero-rating applied.

Wells (1997)

Listed building consent must be required and obtained in order for alterations to be 'approved' and treated as VAT zero-rated.

Alan Roper & Sons Ltd (1997)

In this tribunal, it was confirmed that VAT zero-rating for approved alterations to protected buildings does not apply where listed building consent is granted retrospectively.

Brice (1991)

The tribunal held that in order for construction works to a 'protected building' to be VAT zero-rated, 'approved alterations' must have a written listed building consent from the relevant authority.

C & E Commrs v Arbib (1995)

The owner of a listed farmhouse obtained planning permission and listed building consent for the replacement of a barn with a building to house a swimming pool. The new building was connected to the house by a covered walkway with open sides and a brick wall running between the side of the house and the swimming pool building. It was claimed that the building works fell to be zero-rated, as they were services supplied in the course of an approved alteration of a protected building. This view was supported by the courts.

C & E Commrs v Windflower Housing Association (1995)

This case involved work to the roof of a Grade II listed building. The Housing Association claimed the works were VAT zero-rated, as they comprised alterations to a protected building. Customs disagreed, arguing that the works were repair and maintenance and therefore VAT standard-rated. It was decided by the High Court that the works were repair and maintenance, even though alterations clearly took place. It was a matter of fact and degree, looking at the works as a whole, to decide the correct VAT liability.

Evans (1989)

It was held that the VAT tribunal has regard to the views of the local planning authority (LPA) as to whether a work requires listed building consent, but is not bound by those views.

Hardy (1994)

This case considered the extent to which alterations to an outbuilding to form a family games room and play area could be VAT zero-rated as approved alterations to a protected building. The tribunal held that the outbuilding and main house together did form a 'protected building' and therefore the works could be VAT zero-rated.

[However, the more recent case of *Zielinski Baker & Partners Ltd* does not support this result.]

Heijn (1998)

It was held that the construction of a swimming pool and garden away from a listed dwelling did not qualify as a zero-rated 'approved alteration'.

Walsingham College (Yorkshire Properties) Ltd (1999)

The owner of a listed hall obtained listed building consent for a new sewage treatment plant and claimed zero-rating for the works as approved alterations to a protected building. Customs argued that the works did not require listed building consent and that zero-rating was therefore not possible. However, the tribunal held that listed building consent was indeed required as the sewage system altered the character of the hall.

4.4.2.4 **Listed places of worship**

Many churches and chapels are given special treatment for planning purposes that eliminates the need for listed building consent. This treatment is known as 'ecclesiastical exemption' and applies to selected denominations. The selected denominations in England and Wales are:

- the Church of England;
- the Church in Wales;
- the Roman Catholic Church;

- the Methodist Church;

- the Baptist Union of Great Britain and the Baptist Union of Wales; and

- the United Reformed Church.

In Scotland and Northern Ireland, all listed places of worship (or their equivalent in Northern Ireland) have ecclesiastical exemption.

Listed church buildings that fall under this exemption can be treated as protected buildings for the purposes of the VAT legislation. The listed building consent is replaced by documentation generated by the church concerned. The Church of England issues a document known as a 'faculty'.

A grant scheme known as the 'Listed Places of Worship Grant Scheme' has been introduced. The successful use of the scheme provides a grant to the church concerned to reduce the effective rate of VAT from 17.5% to 0% on repair and maintenance works.

4.4.3 Adaptations for disabled persons

Group 12 of Schedule 8 to the VAT Act 1994 provides that certain goods and services provided to a handicapped person, or to a charity for making these available to handicapped persons, by sale or otherwise, for domestic use or their personal use, can be zero-rated.

'Handicapped' means chronically sick or disabled and covers anyone who is blind, deaf or dumb (and covered by the definition included in the *Chronically Sick and Disabled Persons Act* 1970) or anyone who is substantially and permanently handicapped by illness, injury or congenital deformity.

Since entitlement to zero-rating depends in part on the status of the recipient, zero-rating is only allowed when the recipient gives the supplier an 'eligibility declaration'.

Supplies of specified goods to a charity can also be zero-rated if they are to be made available to handicapped persons. Supplies to hospitals, nursing homes, health authorities, and so on, are not covered, even if they are intended for the disabled, although supplies to handicapped individuals in such establishments are zero-rated.

The following services can benefit from zero-rating:

- The installation of various kinds of hoists and lifts to facilitate the movement of a handicapped person in his or her private residence. Zero-rating also applies to the repair and maintenance of qualifying lifts and hoists.

- The installation of hoists and lifts provided to a charity for making available to handicapped persons by sale or otherwise, for domestic or personal use. Lifts only qualify in the context of permanent or temporary residences, or in day centres for handicapped persons. In other buildings, only chair lifts and stair lifts qualify for the relief. Repair and maintenance are also zero-rated for chair and stair lifts only.

- The construction of ramps, widening of doorways or passageways in a handicapped person's private residence or for a charity to enable a handicapped person to enter or move within any building. This relief covers any preparatory work and making-good work.

- The provision, extension or adaptation of a bathroom, washroom or lavatory in a handicapped person's private residence where this is necessary by reason of the person's condition. This includes related preparatory and making-good works.

- The supply to a handicapped person for domestic or his or her personal use, or to a charity for making available to handicapped persons by sale or otherwise for domestic or their personal use, of alarm systems designed to be capable of operation by a handicapped person, and to enable that person to alert directly a specified person or a control centre. The hiring and the repair and maintenance of eligible equipment and the service of monitoring calls at a control centre are also covered.

- Equipment and appliances not included above, which have been designed solely for use by a handicapped person.

Avis (t/a Property Alterations) (1992)

It was accepted that the construction of a new widened hallway, shower room, new internal doorways and raising of ground outside the patio doors could be VAT zero-rated.

Brand (as Trustee of Racket Sports for Children with Special Needs) (1995)

Works were completed at a tennis club to enable disabled people to use the premises. The works were paid for by the tennis club which was reimbursed by a charity. It was held that the works could not be zero-rated as they had not been paid for by the charity.

Johnson (1999)

It was held that the construction of a conservatory at the home of an arthritis sufferer did not qualify for zero-rating. Works to widen doorways and the provision of access ramps did, however, qualify for zero-rating.

Johnsen (Chairman of Shalden Millennium Committee) (2001)

It was held that works for the construction of new gates and the widening of a gateway were not eligible for zero-rating under Item 9 of Group 12 of Schedule 8 to the VAT Act 1994. The works had been necessary to allow disabled people to be driven to the door of the church rather than walk the 300 yards from the road. The works completed were not covered by the VAT legislation.

Boys' and Girls' Welfare Society (1996)

It was held that special low surface temperature radiators installed at a residential unit for disabled children were only zero-rated where they were installed in bathrooms, washrooms or lavatories. Zero-rating did not apply where they were installed in other areas.

Union of Students of the University of Warwick (1995)

The installation of a lift at a Students Union to enable disabled students to have access to the upper floors was held to be VAT standard-rated. It was held that the campus building failed to qualify as a 'day centre' and thus VAT zero-rating was not available. From 1997, Customs had allowed zero-rating on the installation of lifts for disabled persons in educational institutions. This zero-rating has been withdrawn by Customs as they now consider this treatment was incorrect.

4.5   SUPPLY OF 'RELEVANT GOODS' TO AN 'ELIGIBLE BODY'

Group 15 of Schedule 8 to the VAT Act 1994 provides that the supply of certain 'relevant goods' to an 'eligible body' can be zero-rated. 'Relevant goods' include medical, scientific, computer, video, sterilising, laboratory or refrigeration equipment designed solely for use in medical or veterinary research, training, diagnosis or treatment. In addition, specialist appliances, hoists, and lifters for disabled persons are covered.

For this zero-rating relief to apply, 'relevant goods' must either be supplied for donation to a nominated 'eligible body' or supplied to an 'eligible body' that pays for them with funds provided by a charity.

An 'eligible body' includes health authorities, NHS trusts, charitable institutions providing care or medical or surgical treatment for handicapped persons, not-for-profit research institutions, and hospitals and charitable institutions providing rescue or first aid services.

C & E Commrs v The David Lewis Centre (1995)

The provision of an observation window and padded games room at a charitable residential centre for epilepsy sufferers was held not to qualify as the supply of relevant goods to an eligible body as they were not 'medical goods'.

Royal Midland Counties Home for Disabled People v C & E Commrs (2001)

It was held that the purchase of an emergency generator by a nursing home operated by a charity was 'an accessory for use with medical equipment' and as such qualified for zero-rating as the supply of relevant goods to an eligible body.

Lancer UK Ltd (1986)

Washing machines used for the cleaning of surgical and laboratory equipment were held not to qualify as the supply of relevant goods to an eligible body. It was held that washing machines could be described as scientific equipment.

Severnside Siren Trust Ltd (2000)

The supply of sirens to a charitable trust established to provide and maintain an early warning system for industrial plant fires was held to be VAT zero-rated.

4.6 VAT REDUCED-RATE CONSTRUCTION SERVICES

The emphasis on urban regeneration and energy efficiency has been reflected in the introduction of a number of new 5% VAT reliefs. This includes the introduction from the 2001 Budget onwards of a reduced rate of VAT of 5% for services provided in the following areas:

- residential conversions;

- residential renovations and alterations; and

- the installation and repair of various energy-saving materials and security goods.

4.6.1 Residential conversions

The legislation for residential conversions is contained in Group 6 of Schedule 7A to the VAT Act 1994. Under this new legislation qualifying services provided in the course of qualifying conversions, including any materials provided by the person undertaking the conversion, are chargeable to VAT at 5%. Qualifying services broadly include construction service related to the building and its immediate surroundings but excludes professional fees.

At present, qualifying conversions arise in the following circumstances:

- a conversion resulting in a changed number of dwellings;

- a conversion into a single household dwelling;

- a conversion into a house in multiple occupation; and

- a special residential conversion.

This legislation introduces further definitions associated with residential use of property including the phrases 'single household dwelling' and 'house in multiple occupation'. These phrases and the extent of this VAT relief will no doubt be tested in the courts in due course.

4.6.2 Residential renovations and alterations

The legislation for residential renovations and alterations is contained in Group 7 of Schedule 7A to the VAT Act 1994. It provides that qualifying services, including any materials provided by the person undertaking the renovation or alteration, will be chargeable to VAT at 5%.

At present, qualifying renovations arise in the following circumstances:

- renovation or alteration of 'single household dwellings' that have been empty for three years or more;

- renovation or alteration of buildings used for a 'relevant residential purpose' that have been empty for three years or more;

- renovation or alteration of a multiple-occupancy dwelling that has been empty for three years or more; and

- renovation or conversion of a building to form a garage as part of the renovation of a premises that qualifies for the reduced rate.

Buildings intended for use for 'relevant residential purposes' will require a certificate confirming appropriate usage.

The three-year period must run up to the *beginning* of the renovation or alteration works for the reduced rate to apply. It will be necessary for the contractor to hold evidence to demonstrate that the premises have not been lived in during the three years immediately preceding the works. Customs suggest that such evidence could include electoral roll and council tax data, information from utilities companies, and evidence from empty property officers in local authorities or from other reliable information sources.

Non-residential use and occupation by squatters can be ignored in determining the three-year period.

Monoprio (2002)

This tribunal considered the reduced-rate legislation for building conversions and concerned the 'changed number of dwellings' rules. The tribunal held that some works to create a new dwelling in an outbuilding to a manor house were VAT standard-rated as the first floor of that building already contained a flat which was incorporated into the new premises. There was no change in the number of dwellings and therefore the reduced rate could not apply.

Wellcome Trust (2003)

The meaning of a 'changed number of dwellings conversion' was considered for the first time since the introduction of this legislation in 2001. The owner of two interconnected six-storey terraced houses carried out conversion works to change the number of household dwellings within the premises. Customs issued a ruling that the works to the second-floor level did not qualify, as there was no change in the number of dwellings in that part of the dwelling. The tribunal agreed with this ruling.

Lincoln Oak Company Ltd (2004)

Building materials can only be subject to a reduced rate of VAT where they are supplied by the person undertaking the construction services.

4.6.3 **Energy-saving materials**

From 1 April 2000, the reduced rate of 5% has applied to the installation of qualifying energy-saving materials in all homes including:

- owner-occupied homes;
- homes rented from private landlords;
- homes rented from local authorities and housing associations;
- caravans;
- residential boats;
- residential buildings such as old peoples' homes, children's homes and nursing homes; and
- non-business charity buildings.

Qualifying energy-saving materials

Qualifying energy-saving materials are those that are supplied and installed by a VAT-registered business, and include:

- insulation for walls, floors, ceilings, roofs or lofts, or for water tanks, pipes or other plumbing fittings;
- draught stripping for windows and doors;
- central heating system controls, including thermostatic radiator valves;

- electric dual-immersion water heaters with foam-insulated water tanks;

- hot-water system controls;

- solar panels;

- from 1 June 2004, ground source heat pumps; and

- from 7 April 2005, air source heat pumps and micro combined heat and power units.

Beco Products Ltd and BAG Building Contractors (2004)

It was held that the installation of energy saving blocks in the course of the alteration or extension of an existing building would not benefit from the 5% rate of VAT. Where the blocks were 'installed as part of an entire contract for construction, the dominant purpose of the contract will be the building that results. The dominant purpose will not be the insulation provided by the system ...' The VAT rate was therefore considered to follow the VAT liability of the overall building works in question which, in this case, was 17.5%.

4.6.4 Grant-funded installation of heating equipment, security goods, or connection of gas supply

The installation, repair and maintenance of qualifying heating equipment, security goods and connections for gas supplies, when made to a qualifying person (broadly including pensioners and those in receipt of various government benefits), can be treated at the 5% reduced rate of VAT to the extent that they are funded by qualifying grants schemes.

4.7 DIY HOUSE-BUILDERS AND CONVERTERS

The situation with regard to the zero-rating rules differs slightly for a self-builder to a commercial house-builder.

In the past there was an anomaly with commercial developers broadly suffering no VAT on residential developments, but non-business self-builders unable to recover any VAT on goods purchased to build their own homes. A special refund mechanism is now in place to counter this.

A direct refund of VAT is made by Customs to the self-builder for the VAT incurred on:

- goods purchased to construct a new dwelling – services purchased in the construction of a new dwelling can be zero-rated in the normal way and are therefore not included in the refund process (this could include the services of a bricklayer, plumber or electrician, for example); and

- services utilised in the conversion of a non-residential building to form a new dwelling – these services could be at the standard or reduced rate of VAT, depending on the status of the building prior to the conversion works.

The normal rules apply as to which 'building materials' can benefit from the refund mechanism. In addition, the extent of the refund is similarly restricted to those items classed as forming part of a newly formed dwelling, such as driveways, turfing and fencing, but excluding ornamental garden features and structures such as tennis courts.

This is a one-off claim procedure and therefore care needs to be taken where the completion stage is not distinct or works are to be phased.

Vincett (1993)

It was held that where a builder charged VAT on some works in the course of construction of a house that the DIY builders VAT refund scheme could not authorise a refund of this VAT. The builder should have zero-rated their supplies and as such the individual's remedy was against the builder.

Alexander (1989)

A claim for a refund of VAT by an individual in respect of a newly constructed house attached to an existing residence was rejected because the planning required that the property 'remain solely for the enjoyment of the dwelling house'. It was therefore not a dwelling for the purposes of the VAT legislation.

Flynn (1999)

A claim for a refund of VAT was rejected on the basis that the building being converted was going to be used as a bed and breakfast establishment.

Watson (2003)

A couple who converted a barn into two dwellings made a claim for a refund of VAT under the DIY builder's scheme. It was rejected on the basis that the dwellings were going to be let and therefore the conversion had not been done for non-business purposes. The fact that it was the intention of the couple to allow their young children to occupy the dwellings in ten years time was not relevant.

4.8 SERVICES OF CONSULTANTS

The services of architects, surveyors, engineers, project managers, supervisors and consultants will always be VAT standard-rated at 17.5%. However, in certain circumstances where the contractor completing a development procures the services of consultants, the VAT liability will follow that of the construction services provided that the works proceed on site. If the works only amount to early consultancy advice, they will be VAT standard-rated.

4.9   MISCELLANEOUS MATTERS

Dilapidations

At the end of most leases there is provision for a schedule of dilapidations to be presented to a tenant by his landlord. If a payment is due from the tenant, this takes the form of compensation and is outside the scope of VAT. If the payment is made before the end of the lease, the payment may be considered to be for a taxable supply of services by the landlord.

Business Enterprises (UK) Ltd (1988)

A serviced office provider collected deposit fees from occupiers as payments to cover any dilapidations to the suites. Customs accepted these payments fell outside the scope of VAT as they were not consideration for any supply.

Building control fees

Since the introduction of authorised building control inspectors from the private sector, VAT is charged on all building control fees.

Self-supply of construction services

A deemed VAT supply may arise where a business which cannot recover VAT employs its own direct workforce to carry out construction works and thus avoid VAT on the labour, salary and profit components of the works (the *Value Added Tax (Self-supply of Construction Services) Order* 1989).

These rules apply to construction works, including any preparatory or demolition works carried out at the same time, if any exempt business constructs a building or civil engineering work or extends or alters any building such that an additional floor area of 10% or more is created. The business is deemed both to supply and receive the construction services in question, and it must pay VAT on the deemed self-supply at the open market value.

These rules do not apply if the value of the works is less than £100,000. Any VAT on materials purchased will be recoverable as they relate to the deemed supply of construction services.

Index

abandoned projects
    payment, 13, 14
aborted projects *see* abandoned
        projects
access
    paths, roads, drives, etc., 129
accommodation
    standard-rated
        holiday accommodation, 76,
        77
        hotels, inns, boarding houses,
        73–76
administration *see* collection and
        administration
Agricultural Tenancies Act 1995
    compensation, 58
aircraft
    storage, standard rate, 80
anti-avoidance rules *see* avoidance
        of VAT
approved alterations
    protected buildings *see* protected
        buildings
architects
    place of supply of services, 27
    VAT liability of services, 128, 152
assessments, 49
assignments
    leases, 92, 96, 97
avoidance of VAT, 44–47
    disclosure, 47
    restriction, option to tax, 89–91
    VAT groups, 21, 22
best of commissioners' judgment
    assessment, 49
bicycles
    storage, 78–80
blocked input tax, 43
boarding houses
    accommodation, standard rate,
        73–76
boats
    mooring or storage, standard

rate, 80
breach of regulations
    penalties, 52
building control fees, 153
building materials
    standard rate, 133–136
buildings *see* commercial property;
        construction services; land;
        residential and charitable
        property
business
    case law, 16, 17
    UK perspective, 15, 16
business entertainment
    input tax non-deductible, 43
camping facilities
    standard rate, 77, 78
capital goods scheme, 42, 43
    interaction of taxes, 57
caravans
    seasonal pitches, standard rate,
        77, 78
    storage, 78–80
car parks *see* parking facilities
carpets/carpeting materials, 133
cars
    input tax non-deductible, 43
charitable property *see* residential
        and charitable property
charities
    supply of relevant goods to
        eligible body, 145, 146
*Chronically Sick and Disabled Persons
        Act* 1970, 142
civil engineering works
    definition, 71, 72
    new, sale, 71
civil penalties *see* penalties
collection and administration, 48,
    49
    assessments, 49
    complaints, 55
    disputes

Court of Appeal, 56
European Court of Justice, 57
High Court, 56
House of Lords, 56
local reconsideration, 56
VAT and Duties Tribunal, 56
extra-statutory concessions, 54, 55
penalties, 50
  breach of regulations, 52
  criminal fraud, 51
  default surcharge, 52
  dishonest conduct, 51
  late registration, 52
  misdeclaration, 51, 52
  mitigation, 52
  reasonable excuse, 52, 53
VAT rulings, 53, 54
commercial property
  exempt supplies of land
    election to waive exemption
      see option to tax
    interest in or right over land, 64–67
    leasing or letting of immoveable property, 65–67
    licence to occupy land, 64–70
  lease transactions, 91
    assignments, 92, 96, 97
    inducements, 92, 93
    lease for a premium, 92, 93
    rent-free periods, 92, 95
    reverse assignments, 92, 96, 97
    reverse premiums, 92–94
    reverse surrenders, 92, 95, 96
    service charges, 98, 99
    surrenders, 92, 95, 96
    table of liabilities, 92
    third party costs, 97, 98
    variations to leases, 95, 97
  option to tax see option to tax
  standard-rated supplies of land
    see standard-rated supplies
    of land
  supplies outside the scope of
    VAT, 65

transfer of business as a going
  concern see transfer of
  business as a going
  concern
zero-rated supplies, 64
compensation, 58, 59
complaints, 55
composite supplies see multiple or
  compound supplies
compound supplies see multiple or
  compound supplies
compulsory registration, 18, 19
concert halls
  right to occupy box, seat or other
    accommodation, 80, 81
consideration, 9, 10, 31, 32
  land exchange deals, 10, 11
  supply of services, 13, 14
construction contracts
  liquidated damages, 58
  retention payments, tax point,
    30, 31
construction professionals
  place of supply of services, 27
construction services
  building materials, 133–136
  consultants, 152
  DIY house-builders and
    converters, 150–152
  existing buildings
    adaptations for disabled
      persons, 142–145
    approved alterations to
      protected buildings see
      protected buildings
    housing association
      conversions, 136, 137
    new buildings, 128
    reduced rate see reduced rate
    self-supply, 153, 154
    supply of relevant goods to
      eligible body, 145, 146
    tax point, 30
    works in the course of
      construction, 129–132
consultants
  VAT liability of services, 152

costs
    third party, recovery of VAT, 97,
        98
criminal fraud
    penalties, 51
Crown or Duchy buildings,
    138–141
damages
    compensation, 58, 59
    liquidated, 58
deemed non-supplies
    payments to staff, 9
    transfer of going concern, 9
    VAT groups, 9
deemed supplies
    cases regarding, 8, 9
default surcharge
    late return or payment of VAT, 52
definitions and meanings
    approved alteration, 138
    building, 109–111
    building designed as a dwelling,
        111–114
    building used for a relevant
        charitable purpose, 120–123
    building used for a relevant
        residential purpose,
        118–120
    business, 15, 16
    civil engineering work, 71, 72
    economic activity, 16
    fee simple, 62, 106
    handicapped, 142
    major interest, 62, 105
    non-residential building, 114–118
    protected building, 125
        substantially reconstructed,
        125–127
    supply, 5, 13
    taxable person, 15, 16
    taxable supply, 14
    transfer of a business as a going
        concern, 100
        notifying an election before
        the relevant date, 101, 102
        same kind of business, 101
demolition work, 129

deregistration, 21
development land
    residential see residential and
        charitable property
dilapidations, 153
disabled persons
    adaptations for domestic or
        personal use, 142–145
    handicapped, meaning, 142
discounts
    prompt payment, 33
dishonest conduct
    penalties, 51
disputes
    Court of Appeal, 56
    European Court of Justice, 57
    High Court, 56
    House of Lords, 56
    local reconsideration, 56
    VAT and Duties Tribunal, 56
DIY house-builders and converters,
    150–152
    option to tax, disapplication, 89
drainage, 129
dwellings see also residential and
        charitable property
    option to tax, disapplication, 87,
        88
economic activity
    European perspective, 16
Eighth VAT Directive refunds, 28
equitable right see options
election to waive exemption see
        option to tax
electrical appliances, 133
energy-saving materials
    qualifying, 149, 150
engineers
    VAT liability of services, 152
European Court of Justice
    referral to, 57
European law
    application, 2
    Eighth VAT Directive refunds, 28
    First VAT Directive (77/277), 1
    Second VAT Directive (67/277), 1
    Sixth VAT Directive see Sixth

VAT Directive (77/388)
Thirteenth VAT Directive
refunds, 28
evasion of VAT, 44
dishonest conduct, penalties, 51
exempt supplies, 14
grant of facilities for playing
sport, 81, 82
input tax recovery, 36–39
land see commercial property;
residential and charitable
property
existing buildings
construction services see
construction services
extra-statutory concessions, 54, 55
First VAT Directive (77/277), 1
fishing rights
standard rate, 72, 73
fraud
criminal, penalties, 51
furniture
finished, prefabricated, fitted,
133
gaming rights
standard rate, 72, 73
garages see also parking facilities
constructed at same time as new
dwelling, 114
gas see mains services
gas appliances, 133
goods see supply of goods
grant of a major interest in land, 12
commercial property, 64
major interest, definition,
105–107
residential property, 105
grant of any interest in or right over
land
commercial property, 64–67
residential development land,
103, 104
ground works, 129
group registration
deemed non-supply, 9
handicapped persons see disabled
persons

heating equipment
grant-funded installation,
reduced rate, 150
HM Revenue & Customs, 2
collection and administration see
collection and
administration
holiday accommodation
standard rate, 76, 77
hotel accommodation
standard rate, 73–76
House of Lords
appeals, 56
housing associations
conversions, 136, 137
option to tax, disapplication, 88,
89
Housing (Scotland) Act 1987, 60
Income and Corporation Taxes Act
1988
839, 89
income tax
deduction on account, value of
supply, 34
inducements
leases, 92, 93
inns
accommodation, standard rate,
73–76
input tax, 3
non-deductible, 43, 44
recovery, 34, 35
blocked, 43
capital goods scheme, 42, 43
non-business activities, 35, 36
partial exemption, 39–41
taxable or exempt activities,
36–39
insolvency, 47, 48
installed goods
place of supply, 26
intending traders
registration, 19, 20
interaction of taxes, 57
stamp duty land tax, 57
joint and several liability
VAT groups, 22

joint ventures, 11, 12
land
   residential and charitable
      property *see* residential and
      charitable property
   commercial property *see*
      commercial property
   exchange deals, consideration,
      10, 11
   grant of a major interest in land,
      12
      commercial property, 64
      major interest, definition,
         105–107
      residential property, 105
   grant of any interest in or right
      over land
      commercial property, 64–67
      residential development land,
         103, 104
   licence to occupy land
      commercial property, 64–70
      residential development land,
         103, 104
   related services, place of supply,
      27
   standard-rated supplies *see*
      standard-rated supplies of
      land
Landlord and Tenant Act 1954
   compensation, 58
landscaping, 129
late registration
   penalties, 52
leases *see* commercial property;
   residential and charitable
   property
leasing or letting of immoveable
   property
   commercial property, 65–67
legislation *see* European law; *Value
   Added Tax Act* 1994; *Value
   Added Tax Regulations* 1995
   (SI 1995/2518)
licence to occupy land
   commercial property, 64–70

residential development land,
   103, 104
liquidated damages, 58
listed buildings *see* protected
   buildings
local authorities and other
   governmental bodies,
   59–62
local reconsideration
   disputes, 56
mains services, 129
major interest in land *see* grant of a
   major interest in land
meanings *see* definitions and
   meanings
misdeclaration
   penalties, 51, 52
mitigation
   civil penalties, 52
mobile offices, 129
moorings
   ships, boats or other vessels, 80
multiple or compound supplies, 22
   composite supplies, 23, 24
   current test, 22, 23
   multiple supplies, 24, 25
new buildings
   construction services *see*
      construction services
new commercial buildings
   civil engineering, definition, 71,
      72
   sale of, 71
new dwellings
   certain items where input tax
      non-deductible, 44
non-business activities
   case law, 17, 18
   input tax recovery, 35, 36
non-residential building
   definition, 114–118
   housing association conversions,
      136, 137
non-supplies *see* deemed non-
   supplies
options
   standard rate, 82

option to tax, 70
 disapplication, 87, 103
  anti-avoidance restriction,
   89–91
  dwellings, 87, 88
  housing associations, 88, 89
  self-builders, 89
  test, 89
  utilisation, 47
 making, 84–86
 notifying an election before the
  relevant date, meaning,
  101, 102
 principles, 82–84
 residential development land,
  103, 104
output tax, 3
outside the scope of VAT, 14
 commercial property, 65
 compensation, 58
parking facilities
 standard rate, 78–80
partial exemption
 recovery of input tax, 39–41
partnerships, 11, 12
payment of VAT
 late, default surcharge, 52
payments to staff
 deemed non-supply, 9
penalties, 50
 breach of regulations, 52
 criminal fraud, 51
 default surcharge, 52
 dishonest conduct, 51
 late registration, 52
 misdeclaration, 51, 52
 mitigation, 52
 reasonable excuse, 52, 53
personal right see options
physical recreation see sports
  facilities
pitches
 caravans/tents, standard rate,
  77, 78
place of supply
 supplies of goods, 25, 26
 supplies of services, 27, 28

places of worship
 listed, 141, 142
plant and machinery, 129
pre-emption right see options
pre-fabricated furniture, 133
pre-registration VAT
 recovery, 20
profit sharing agreements, 11
project managers
 place of supply of services, 27
 VAT liability of services, 152
property see commercial property;
  residential and charitable
  property
protected buildings, 137, 138
 approved alterations, 137, 138
 Crown or Duchy buildings,
  138–141
 listed places of worship, 141,
  142
 meaning, 125
 substantially reconstructed,
  meaning, 125–127
protection of the revenue
 VAT grouping, refusal, 22
reasonable excuse
 penalties, 52, 53
recovery of VAT see also input tax
 pre-registration expenditure, 20
 restrictions, 4
 third party costs, 97, 98
reduced rate
 construction services, 128, 146
 energy-saving materials, 149
 grant-funded installation of
  heating equipment,
  security goods or
  connection of gas supply,
  150
 residential conversions, 147
 residential renovations and
  alterations, 147–149
refund of VAT
 Eighth VAT Directive
  refunds, 28
 Thirteenth VAT Directive
  refunds, 28

registration
 compulsory, 18, 19
 deregistration, 21
 intending trader, 19, 20
 late, penalties, 52
 pre-registration VAT, 20
 voluntary, 19
regulatory breaches
 penalties, 52
relevant charitable purpose *see*
  residential and charitable
  property
relevant residential purpose *see*
  residential and charitable
  property
rent-free periods, 92, 95
residential and charitable property,
  103
 building, definition, 109–111
 building designed as a dwelling,
  definition, 111–114
 garages, 114
 building used for a relevant
  charitable purpose,
  definition, 120–123
 charitable annexe, 123, 124
 building used for a relevant
  residential purpose,
  definition, 118–120
 change of qualifying use, 127
 construction services *see*
  construction services
 non-residential building,
  definition, 114–118
 option to tax, disapplication,
  87–89
 person constructing building,
  108, 109
 residential development land,
  103, 104
 sale and letting of residential
  property, 105
 substantially reconstructed
  protected building *see*
  protected buildings
 supply of first grant of major
  interest, 64

residential conversions
 reduced rate, 147
residential renovations and
  alterations
 reduced rate, 147–149
retention payments
 tax point, 30, 31
returns, 3, 4
 late, default surcharge, 52
reverse assignments
 leases, 92, 96, 97
reverse charge, 27
reverse premiums
 leases, 92–94
reverse surrenders
 leases, 92, 95
road fuel
 input tax non-deductible, 43
Scottish law, 62, 63, 106
seasonal pitches
 caravans, standard rate, 77, 78
Second VAT Directive (67/277), 1
security goods
 grant-funded installation,
  reduced rate, 150
self-builders *see* DIY house-builders
  and converters
self-supply
 construction services, 153, 154
service charges, 98, 99
services *see* supply of services
Sheldon statement, 54, 55
ships
 mooring or storage, standard
  rate, 80
Sixth VAT Directive
  (77/388), 1, 2
 art. 4, 15
 art. 4(1), 16, 17
 art. 4(5), 60
 art. 13B, 83
 art. 13B(b), 65; 70
 art. 13B(g), (h), 65
sports facilities
 grant for playing sport
  exemption, 81, 82
 standard rate, 81, 82

sports grounds
   right to occupy box, seat or other
      accommodation, 80, 81
stamp duty land tax (SDLT)
   interaction of taxes, 57
standard-rated supplies of land, 64,
   70
   construction services *see*
      construction services
   grant of facilities for playing
      sport, 81, 82
   holiday accommodation, 76, 77
   hotels and similar
      accommodation, 73–76
   options, 82
   provision of parking facilities,
      78–80
   right to fell or remove timber, 80
   right to take game or fish, 72, 73
   sale of new commercial
      buildings, 71
      civil engineering, definition,
         71, 72
   seasonal pitches for caravans,
      tents or camping facilities,
      77, 78
   seats at sports grounds, theatre,
      concert halls, etc., 80, 81
   storage or aircraft and boats, 80
standing timber
   right to fell or remove, standard
      rate, 80
storage
   standard-rated
      aircraft and boats, 80
      caravans and bicycles, 78–80
supervisors
   VAT liability of services, 152
supply
   cases regarding deemed
      supplies, 8, 9
   cases where held that no supply
      made, 6–8
   cases where held that supply
      made, 5, 6
   consideration, 9, 10
   land exchange deals, 10, 11

deemed non-supplies
   payments to staff, 9
   transfer of going concern, 9
   VAT groups, 9
deemed supplies, cases regarding,
   8, 9
definition, 5, 13

   supply of goods, 12, 13
   place of supply, 25, 26
   possession, meaning, 13
   supply, meaning, 13
   tax point, 29
supply of services, 13, 14
   place of supply, 27, 28
   tax point, 29
surrenders
   leases, 92, 95, 96
surveyors
   place of supply of services, 27
   VAT liability of services, 128, 152
swimming pools, 129
taxable person
   case law
      business, 16, 17
      non-business, 17, 18
   definition, UK and European
      legislation, 15
      European perspective,
         economic activity, 16
      UK perspective, business, 15,
         16
   registration *see* registration
   VAT groups, 21, 22
taxable supplies, 14, 15
   input tax recovery, 36–39
tax avoidance, 45
tax deductions
   value of supply, 34
tax mitigation, 44, 45
tax point, 28–30
   construction services, 30
   retention payments, 30, 31
tennis courts, 129
tents
   pitches / camping facilities,
      standard rate, 77, 78

theatres
   right to occupy box, seat or other
      accommodation, 80, 81
third party costs
   recovery of VAT, 97, 98
Thirteenth VAT Directive refunds,
   28
timber
   standing, right to fell or remove,
      80
time limits
   assessments, 49, 50
time of supply *see* tax point
transfer of business as a going
   concern
   deemed non-supply, 9
   generally, 99, 100
   meaning, 100
   notifying an election before the
      relevant date, meaning,
      101, 102
   same kind of business, meaning,
      101
valuation of supplies *see* value of
   supply
value added tax, 1
   basic operation, 3
      input tax, 3
      output tax, 3
      recovery of VAT, restrictions, 4
      returns, 3, 4
   main charging provision, 4
Value Added Tax Act 1994, 2
   s. 4(1), 4
   s. 5(2), 5
   s. 33, 59–61
   s. 41, 59
   s. 89, 31, 32
   96, 106
   96(1), 105, 106
   Sch. A1, para. 1(7), 18
   Sch. 4, 12
   Sch. 7A, Grp. 6, 147
   Sch. 7A, Grp. 7, 147
   Sch. 8, Grp. 5, item 2, 128
   Sch. 8, Grp. 5, item 3, 136
   Sch. 8, Grp. 5, item 4, 133

Sch. 8, Grp. 5, Note (2), 107, 111,
   112, 114–116
Sch. 8, Grp. 5, Note (2)(a), 113
Sch. 8, Grp. 5, Note (2)(c), (d),
   114
Sch. 8, Grp. 5, Note (3), 114
Sch. 8, Grp. 5, Note (4), 118, 119
Sch. 8, Grp. 5, Note (6), 120
Sch. 8, Grp. 5, Note (6)(a), 120
Sch. 8, Grp. 5, Note (6)(b), 122
Sch. 8, Grp. 5, Note (7), 114–116
Sch. 8, Grp. 5, Note (9), 117, 118
Sch. 8, Grp. 5, Note (13), 107
Sch. 8, Grp. 5, Note (16)–(18),
   109, 110
Sch. 8, Grp. 5, Note (16), 123
Sch. 8, Grp. 5, Note (17), 123, 124
Sch. 8, Grp. 5, Note (21), 136
Sch. 8, Grp. 5, Note (22), 133, 135
Sch. 8, Grp. 6, item 2, 137
Sch. 8, Grp. 6, Note (1), 125
Sch. 8, Grp. 6, Note (4), 125, 126
Sch. 8, Grp. 6, Note (6), 138
Sch. 8, Grp. 12, 142
Sch. 8, Grp. 12, item 9, 144
Sch. 8, Grp. 15, 145
Sch. 9, Grp. 1, item 1, 65, 70, 103
Sch. 10, para. 1, 127
Sch. 10, para. 2, 103
Sch. 10, para. 3, 85
Value Added Tax Regulations 1995 (SI
   1995/2518), 2
   reg. 108, 36
   reg. 109, 36
*Value Added Tax (Self-supply of
   Construction Services) Order
   1989 (SI 1989/472), 153
value of supply, 31–33
   discounts, 33
   tax deductions, 34
variations to leases, 95, 97
VAT and Duties Tribunal
   appeals to, 56
VAT avoidance *see* avoidance of
   VAT
VAT groups, 21, 22
   deemed non-supplies, 9

VAT returns *see* returns
VAT rulings, 53, 54
vessels
    mooring or storage, standard
      rate, 80
voluntary registration, 19

zero-rated supplies
    adaptations for disabled persons,
      142, 143
    commercial property, 64
    construction services, 128